86-01783

J270.092
TWO
        Twomey, Mark J.

A Parade of saints.

Withdrawn

A PARADE OF SAINTS

A PARADE

OF SAINTS

by

Mark J. Twomey

illustrated by

Placid Stuckenschneider, O.S.B.

The Liturgical Press

Collegeville   Minnesota

Acknowledgements

It is a pleasure to thank all who assisted in the research and preparation of *A Parade of Saints*. We are grateful to our colleagues at The Liturgical Press for their advice in writing, designing, editing, and publishing this book . . . to Sr. Colette Primus, O.S.B., St. Benedict's Convent, St. Joseph, Minnesota; Sr. Benedette Rheude, S.S.N.D., Providence Manor, Holy Trinity, Alabama; and to Fr. Michael Kwatera, O.S.B., St. John's Abbey, Collegeville, Minnesota, for evaluating and encouraging this project . . . to Judy, Joseph, Jonathan, and Lisa Twomey, the author's wife and children, for their advice on organizing and presenting this parade . . . and to *The St. Cloud Visitor*, St. Cloud, Minnesota, for permission to reprint a number of the illustrations, which had initially been published in this diocesan paper.

Library of Congress Cataloging in Publication Data

Twomey, Mark J. (Mark Joseph), 1937–
    A parade of saints.
    Summary: Forty-two stories providing biographies of fifty-two saints who gave special service and love to God and man.
    1. Christian saints—Biography—Juvenile literature. [1. Saints] I. Stuckenschneider, Placid, ill. II. Title.
BX4658.T88 1983   270'092'2[B] [920] 82-20397
ISBN 0-8146-1275-X

Nihil obstat: Robert C. Harren. *Censor deputatus. Imprimatur:* ✠George H. Speltz, D.D., Bishop of St. Cloud, Minnesota. September 13, 1982.

CONTENTS

INTRODUCTION

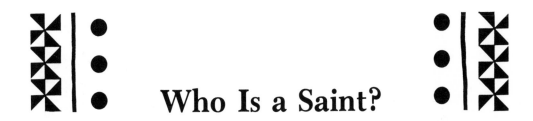

Who Is a Saint?

These stories and illustrations describe about fifty of God's people whom we now remember as saints. Some of the men and women in this parade of saints lived centuries ago. Others lived in this century. Some lived to be wise and old, while others died in the prime of life. Some were popes or served popes. Others tilled the fields or fished the seas. Some were short and stocky, while others were tall and thin. Some are angels, who have always lived with God in eternity. These saints all enjoyed one important achievement—their lives gave proof of special service and love of God and their neighbor.

Everyone who has ever lived belongs to God's people. Thus it is possible for any person to be a saint. Pope John Paul II has told us that "all are called to sanctity, no one is excluded." Daily boys and girls and men and women, whose lives on earth may or may not have called for cheering and fanfare, march into heaven as saints.

Only God knows just how many people have qualified for sainthood. That is why on November 1, All Saints Day, we honor all the saints who have ever lived. On other feast days throughout the year, we remember in a particular way certain people of God whose lives of service and love have told us that they are saints.

How Is a Person Named a Saint?

How does the Church name a person a saint? Centuries ago Christians were often persecuted, even killed, simply because they loved Jesus. The Christians who survived the persecutions then proclaimed the martyrs saints. Later, when the persecutions stopped, the Christians named as saints those people of God who had lived exceptional lives of holiness and goodness.

In time, the local bishop, after carefully studying the candidate's life, decided whether or not a particular person of God should be named a saint. The bishop would then assign a certain day of the year as the feast day of the new saint. Over the years the bishops often asked the Pope, the head bishop, whether or not a person should be canonized, that is, named a saint (the word *saint* comes from the Latin *sanctus,* meaning "holy"). Eventually, then, the Pope, after reviewing the evidence about the candidates, would decide on every case. The first saint to be canonized by a pope was St. Ulric. The year was 993.

Today, over nine hundred years later, the process of naming a saint has remained basically the same. Individuals and groups interested in having a certain person considered for sainthood work with the local bishop in preparing a lengthy report as to why this person should be canonized. The bishop then sends that report to an office of the Church in Rome, Italy, called the Congregation for the Causes of Saints. There officials, including bishops and cardinals, continue the investigation and advise the Pope whether or not the candidate should be named a saint.

Beatification and Canonization

The procedure has several steps. The Congregation studies reports presented to it concerning the heroic virtues of the candidate. Regarding such virtues, Pope Benedict XV said: "Even the most simple works performed with constant perfection in the midst of inevitable difficulties spell heroism in any servant of God." After accepting the report about the candidate, the Holy Father names the person a "venerable."

Besides gathering reports about the virtues of the candidate, the Congregation conducts elaborate investigations to learn if miracles have occurred because of the person's intercession with God. Usually after two miracles have been certified, the Pope at a "beatification" ceremony at St. Peter's Basilica declares the candidate a *beatus* (*beata,* f.) or "blessed." The Pope then uncovers a photo or a painting of the blessed person. The people of the city, region, or religious Order of the blessed person are encouraged to pray to him or her, asking for the blessed's intercession with God.

The investigation about miracles continues. In most cases, when two miraculous cures have been proven due to the blessed's intercession with God, the Holy Father, at a solemn ceremony called a canonization, declares to the world that the blessed is a saint in heaven. Miracles are not required for martyrs. In the Mass celebrated at the ceremony, the Pope for that one day mentions the new saint in the Eucharistic Prayer, what was formerly called the *Canon* of the Mass.

In recent years the Church has somewhat relaxed its long-standing requirements about miracles being certified. It now seems sufficient that the Congregation for the Causes of Saints learns that there is a well-established belief among the people of God that miracles have occurred through the candidate's intercession with God.

Formerly, the procedure moved very slowly, usually taking many years (changes announced in 1983 have reduced the time to as little as ten years). The case of St. John Neumann, the United States' third saint, was typical. Bishop Neumann died in 1860. In 1921 Pope Benedict XV named him a venerable. In 1963 Pope Paul VI declared him a blessed, and in 1977 the same Pope canonized John Neumann a saint.

Certain miracles convinced the Congregation for the Causes of Saints and the Pope that God had answered prayers through the bishop's intercession. In 1923, Eva Benassi of Sassuolo, Italy, was cured of acute peritonitis after a nun asked people to pray to Venerable Neumann. The sister touched a photo of the bishop to Eva's swollen stomach. The infection, which soon would have killed her, disappeared that night.

Years later, in 1949, nineteen-year-old J. Kent Lanahan of Villanova, Pennsylvania, was seriously injured in a car accident. He suffered a crushed skull, a broken collarbone, and a punctured lung. The doctors could do nothing for him. He was unconscious with a 107-degree fever. A neighbor lent Ken's parents a piece of Bishop Neumann's cassock. They touched the bit of cloth to their son, and a little while later Kent recovered.

In 1963, six-year-old Michael Flanagan of West Philadelphia had six months to live because of an incurable bone cancer called Ewing's sarcoma. His parents carried Michael several times to St. Peter's Church in Philadelphia, where the bishop's body lies in view under an altar, and prayed at his tomb. Six months after the diagnosis of this incurable cancer, Michael had no signs of the disease.

On June 19, 1977, Eva, Kent, and Michael were among the twenty thousand joyful people in St. Peter's Square to witness Pope Paul VI announce to the world that Bishop Neumann is a saint.

1. Saints of the Americas

BLESSED

KATERI

TEKAKWITHA

LILY
OF THE
MOHAWKS

Blessed Kateri Tekakwitha

Three hundred years ago the Mohawk village of Ossernenon in upstate New York was not the tranquil, rural community that it is today. It was then on the outermost edge of the known world. There Indians struggled to eke out a living from field and forest. Smallpox and other dreaded diseases often ravaged their lodges during the long and bitter winters.

Over one such winter, smallpox claimed the lives of the parents and the little brother of a four-year-old Mohawk girl named Tekakwitha. She survived that fever, but not without damage. Her face was pockmarked and her eyesight permanently dimmed.

Tekakwitha's uncle, chief of the Mohawk clan named the Turtles, liked his niece and took her into his family. He ordered his braves to burn the disease-infested lodges of Ossernenon to the ground. Then the clan moved a few miles up the Mohawk River to a place called Kanawake.

Blessed Kateri Tekakwitha

b. 1656

d. April 17, 1680

Meaning of name — pure, from the Greek *katharôs*

Feast Day — July 14

Iroquois	Kati	Cass
Kateri	Katharina	Cassie
	Katarina	Kathleen
Latin, Portuguese		Katharine
Catharina	*Norwegian*	Katherine
	Karen	
French		Kathryn
Catherena	*English*	Karen
Katrine	Catherine	Kassia
	Catharine	Katina
Spanish	Cathleen	Katinka
Catalina	Cat	Kate
	Cathy	Kati
Italian	Catty	Kathe
Caterina	Caren	Kay
	Caron	Kaye
German	Carine	Kit
Katrin	Carine	Kit
Käthe	Catarine	Kitty

What is the origin or root of a name? Just about every English name originated centuries ago in one of four parent languages or language groups—Greek, Hebrew and Aramaic (of the Hebrew people), Latin (of the Romans), or the Germanic languages of northern Europe.

The name box to some extent points out how the given saint's name derived from the parent language. For example, a French missionary, using the alphabet of the Iroquois language, renamed the Lily of the Mohawks *Kateri* after St. Catherine. That name derives from the Greek *katharôs*, which means "pure." (In Iroquois Kateri's original name *Tekakwitha* means "one who puts things in order.") The English listing includes borrowings from other languages that are in common use. The box also lists the various diminutives or nicknames of that particular name. By no means is the list for any name complete.

While the spelling of a name may be the same in two or more languages, the pronunciation may differ. For example, "Robert" in French is pronounced Ro-BEAR and in Norwegian something close to Ro-BERT.

m. and f. refer to the masculine and feminine use of a name.

13

Tekakwitha was no burden to her uncle's family in this new community. Her aunt taught her to plant and cultivate corn, to gather berries, to cook the game killed by the hunters. Using porcupine quills as needles, Tekakwitha daintily embroidered designs in beads on deerskin leggings and moccasins. Her nimble fingers, artistic sense, and skillful use of color made Tekakwitha's handiwork admired throughout the village.

In 1667 three Jesuit blackrobes visited Kanawake, where Tekakwitha's uncle warmly hosted them for three days. While Tekakwitha served meals to these guests, she overheard with interest the missionaries' conversation about Christianity. She then recalled from her earliest memory the stories about Jesus that her own mother, a Christian Algonquin, had told her before Tekakwitha was orphaned. The priests could not help but notice Tekakwitha's interest in their religion. But to her uncle this new religion was not a popular subject. He expected the Turtles to follow the traditional beliefs of the Mohawks.

Some years passed and Tekakwitha was now seventeen, an age for an Indian maiden to long be married. Her uncle could not understand why she refused to marry. An unmarried woman was unheard of among the Mohawks, since survival depended upon the support of a husband. He had hoped that Tekakwitha would wed the handsome brave Two Feathers. This strong Mohawk would then help his father-in-law hunt and fish, and Two Feathers would eventually become the next chief of the Turtles.

Little did Tekakwitha's uncle know that his niece had decided never to marry. Worse yet in the chief's eyes, Tekakwitha wanted to be baptized. "My mother was a Christian and I want to be one too," she told Fr. Jacques de Lamberville, the priest at the Jesuit mission at Kanawake.

On Easter Sunday, 1676, Tekakwitha realized her wish. Father de Lamberville baptized her Kateri, which is Iroquois for Catherine. Both Kateri and the priest knew that from then on life would no longer be pleasant for the new Christian in the chief's

house. Before long it became clear that it was unsafe for Kateri to remain in Kanawake. Her relatives threw stones at her. On Sundays, the Lord's Day, when Kateri refused to work in the fields, her aunt would not give her a bite to eat. Also, her aunt spread vicious false stories about Kateri's character throughout the village.

Father de Lamberville, not wanting Kateri to endure this cruel treatment any longer, arranged for her to flee Kanawake. With two other Christian Indians, Kateri that fall of 1677 traveled on foot and by canoe the hundred miles to the Christian Indian settlement of Caughnawaga, not far from Montreal on the St. Lawrence River. Kateri's uncle was furious about the flight of his niece, but he could take little action against her. Kateri was out of his reach.

On Christmas Day, 1677, Kateri received her first Holy Communion. In Caughnawaga Kateri continued to plant and to harvest the crops, to sew at her handiwork, to work much as she had done in Kanawake. But now she was free to visit the chapel daily and to live her Christian faith without fear. The missionary Fr. Pierre Cholenec, one of Kateri's biographers, wrote that she was "not one of those obstinate devotees who are in church when they should be at home."

Father Cholenec spoke of Kateri as the "miracle of our forests." He noticed that the other-worldliness that had grown more and more into her character did not alienate the people from her. She walked her simple way among them, helping with the sick, caring for the children, performing insofar as she was able any work of charity that offered itself.

Despite one sickness after the other, Kateri was cheerful and kept up with her duties as far as possible. She had trouble with her eyes, constant headaches, and, in the year that she died, "a stomach ailment . . . which was accompanied by vomiting and finally by a low fever." Such frail health led to Kateri's death when she was but twenty-four. On her deathbed on the Wednesday of Holy Week in 1680, Kateri told a dear friend, "I will love you in heaven; I will pray for you; I will assist you."

Indeed, Kateri has been an intercessor with God for many since she died. Soon after she was buried in Caughnawaga, both the Indians and the French settlers flocked to her grave in pilgrimage. Even the bishop of Quebec City, Jean de St. Vallier, prayed at her grave. A missionary wrote that "members of our French population . . . flock from all sides to the tomb of the servant of God, Kateri Tekakwitha."

Kateri's biographers have detailed many cures attributed to this holy maiden's intercession with God. But apart from such possible miracles, in 1932 the Church opened the cause for Kateri's sanctity because of the written record of Kateri's virtuous life left by the Jesuit missionaries. Kateri lived the message of the Gospels to the fullest, sharing her talents and cheerfulness with others and offering her suffering as an unending prayer to God.

In 1943, Pope Pius XII declared Kateri Tekakwitha a venerable. The long road to sainthood for Kateri advanced another major step on June 22, 1980, when she was beatified. There in St. Peter's Basilica in Rome, five hundred North American Indians from thirty-five tribes, along with twenty-five thousand people from around the world, witnessed Pope John Paul II declare Kateri, as well as four other venerables, a blessed. That day the Indians' splendid leather attire, decorated with sequins and beads, was reminiscent of the handiwork that Blessed Kateri herself had crafted three centuries earlier.

It is probable that the Lily of the Mohawks, as Blessed Kateri Tekakwitha is often called, will be canonized the next American saint. She is the first American Indian as well as the first American layperson to be beatified.

The national shrine to Blessed Kateri is at Fonda, New York, the site of the Mohawk village of Kanawake, where Kateri was baptized.

St. Elizabeth Ann Seton

St. Elizabeth Ann Seton, sometimes called Mother Seton, the first native-born American citizen to be canonized a saint, was not a "born Catholic." She was the daughter of a wealthy Episcopalian family in New York City. Her relatives, by blood or by marriage, included families of fame and power in the colonial United States. She grew up next door to Alexander Hamilton.

Elizabeth Ann Bayley was born in 1774, two years before the United States itself was born. Her father remained a loyalist during the Revolutionary War and served as a surgeon to the British Redcoats who fought George Washington's militiamen.

When Elizabeth was yet a little girl, her mother died, but her father saw to it that his daughter received the best education possible in the colonies. As a schoolgirl Elizabeth looked forward to the time when she could care for the sick, especially those who were poor.

In 1794, when she was twenty, Elizabeth married William Seton. They became the parents of five children. Besides looking after her husband and family, Elizabeth established an organization in New York City called the Widows' Society. She and other members daily visited the poor in their homes to nurse and comfort them. Little did Elizabeth know that she would soon become a widow and with her children face sad and difficult times.

St. Elizabeth Ann Seton

b. August 28, 1774
d. January 4, 1821
Founder of the American Sisters of Charity

Feast Day — January 4

Meaning of name — consecrated to God, from the Hebrew *elisheba*

French
Élisabeth
Élisa
Élise
Lise
Lisette
Belle

Spanish
Isabel

Italian
Elisa
Elisabetta

German
Elisabeth
Elisa

Russian
Ylizaeta

Norwegian
Elisabet

English
Elizabeth
Elisabeth
Eliza
Elsa
Elsie
Elspeth
Elyse
Babette

Batya
Bess
Bessie
Belle
Bella
Bette
Betty
Betsey
Bettina
Bethia
Bithia
Isabel
Isabella
Ilse
Isa
Ib
Lee
Libby
Lilibet
Lilla
Lillah
Lisa
Lise
Liz
Liza
Lizette
Lizzy
Tetsey
Tetty
Tibbie

16

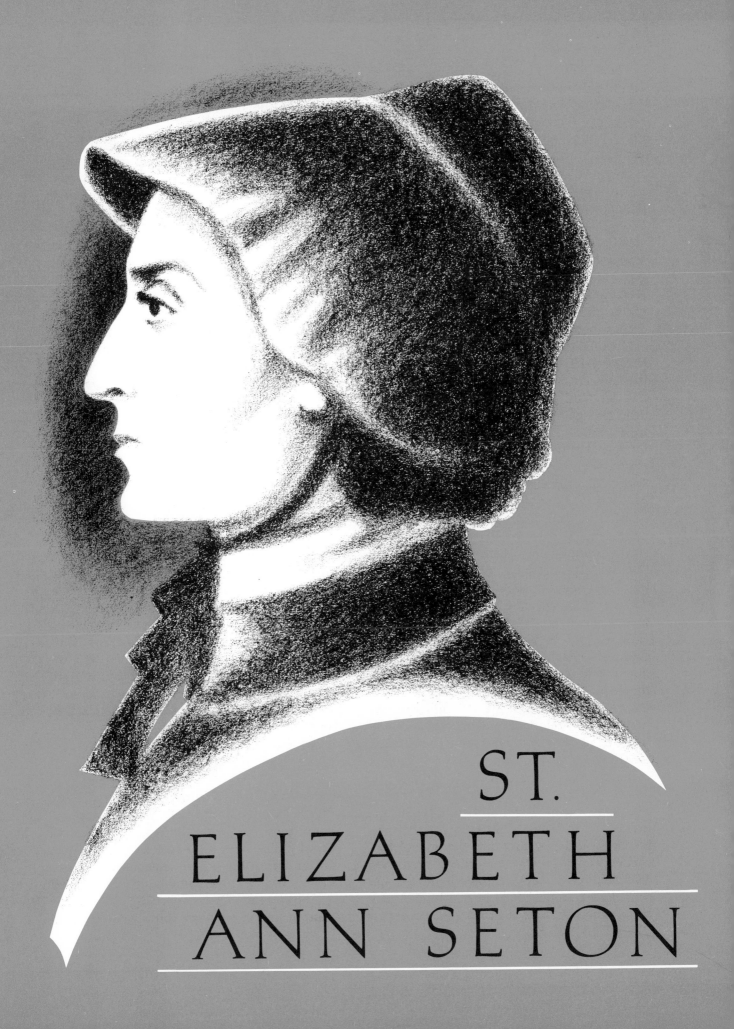

ST.
ELIZABETH
ANN SETON

The Seton family's shipping business went bankrupt when many ships were lost at sea during wars. Most of the crews and cargoes of the Seton fleet were at the bottom of the Atlantic. To make matters worse, William Seton became seriously ill with tuberculosis, which was a dreaded killer in those days. The couple and their oldest daughter Anna moved to sunny Italy, where William hoped to regain his health. But instead of recovering, he died shortly after the long sea voyage. Family friends of the Setons, the Filicchis, who were Catholics, helped Elizabeth through these difficult times. Eventually Elizabeth returned to New York City determined to become a Catholic.

In 1805, having completed instructions in her new faith, Elizabeth was received into the Church. She was happy to be a Catholic, but her family of devout Episcopalians was dead set against Elizabeth's decision. At that time, unlike today, people were often very intolerant of other religions. Elizabeth's close relatives chose to forget that they had ever known her and would not lend her money or help her pay her bills.

Elizabeth was now a destitute widow with no means to care for her children. It was almost impossible to make ends meet. The bills were piling up. Elizabeth had to work night and day to make a simple living for her children. She started a school, but that soon closed when students would not come to class simply because their teacher was a Catholic. Elizabeth next set up a boarding house and cooked, sewed, and mothered fourteen boys who attended school elsewhere in the city. But life was still very difficult for the Setons. Elizabeth was seriously thinking about moving her family to Canada, where she hoped life would be easier.

Fortunately, Elizabeth did not have to make that move. A priest in Baltimore, Maryland, learned of Elizabeth's plight and invited her to begin a girls' school in that city. Elizabeth did just that and the school succeeded, though it was not without problems. The next year, 1809, Elizabeth moved her school to a stone house in nearby Emmitsburg, where in time it prospered. Poor girls who could pay no tuition as well as wealthy girls attended this school. This was the beginning of the Order of sisters that Elizabeth founded.

On March 25 that spring, a priest-friend, Fr. William Dubourg, with the blessing of Bishop John Carroll of Baltimore, witnessed Elizabeth's first promises as a religious. Father Dubourg gave her the title of "Mother." Indeed, the title was especially appropriate for Elizabeth. Some of her own children were still at the Stone House with her, and she was now the superior of the women who joined her Order.

That June the sisters started wearing a religious habit. They called themselves the Sisters of St. Joseph. By January, 1812, twenty women, including Elizabeth's sisters-in-law Harriet and Cecilia, had joined her community. They decided to follow the rule of the Sisters of Charity in France.

Mother Seton wrote textbooks, translated books from French to English, trained teachers, and wrote articles on the spiritual life. As in earlier years with the Widows' Society, Elizabeth continued to visit the sick and the poor of the neighborhood. The sisters brought them medicine, food, and clothes, cleaned their homes, cared for the children, and offered kind words of encouragement.

In 1814 her sisters started a home in Philadelphia and cared for the children at St. Joseph's Orphanage. Three years later they opened an orphanage in New York City, Mother Seton's hometown. Wherever the sisters worked, they taught school. Thus, Mother Seton is sometimes considered a founder of the American parochial school system.

Mother Seton died in 1821, but the work of her sisters has steadily grown over the last 160 years. Today six separate communities of sisters trace their beginning to Emmitsburg. Five of these communities are now independently organized and are called Sisters of Charity. The sixth is the American Daughters of Charity. In 1850 these sisters united with a French Order of the same name. That Order is the largest Order of religious in the Church, in 1982 having thirty-two thousand members across the world. The motherhouse or headquarters of the Order is in Paris, France. In the United States the Daughters of Charity staff hospitals, child-care institutions, homes for the aged and handicapped, and schools at every level.

Those who knew Mother Seton realized that it was only a matter of time before she would be canonized a saint. In 1882 James Cardinal Gibbons of Baltimore took the first step toward having Elizabeth so honored. The Church then officially began a detailed study of her life with that cause in mind. The officials learned that at least three miracles have been attributed to Elizabeth's intercession with God. A child was miraculously cured of leukemia, a woman was similarly cured of cancer, and a man recovered miraculously from a massive brain infection.

In 1959 Pope John XXIII declared Mother Seton a venerable, and in 1963 a blessed. Then, on September 14, 1975, Pope Paul VI named Elizabeth Seton a saint of the Church. She became the first native-born American to be canonized.

The saint's body rests beneath an altar in the chapel of the National Shrine of St. Elizabeth Seton in Emmitsburg, Maryland, which is located in the provincial house (headquarters) of the Daughters of Charity of the Emmitsburg Province.

St. John Neumann

John Nepomucene Neumann could not be ordained a priest in his native Czechoslovakia in the 1830s because there were enough priests. Seminarians in that country had to wait a year or more after finishing their education to be ordained. From missionary priests serving in the United States, John had heard of the great need for priests to work in the German-speaking parishes of New York. Thus, in 1836 John sailed for New York City. He had only a few coins in his pocket and no certain future other than his desire to be ordained a priest and to work where he was needed.

God had great plans for John Neumann. He would admirably serve parishes in several cities of his adopted country. He would become the fourth bishop of Philadelphia. And in 1977 the Church would name him a saint, the third American and the first male American to be canonized.

Neumann was born in Prachatitz, Czechoslovakia, in 1811. His parents named him after the patron saint of that country, John Nepomucene, a priest who was murdered by cruel King Wenceslaus in the fourteenth century. John's well-to-do parents sent their son to Czechoslovakia's best schools, including the seminary at Budweis. Although John finished his seminary studies in 1835, he could not be ordained immediately.

He therefore wrote to Bishop John Dubois of the diocese of New York, which then covered all of New York state and part of New Jersey. John volunteered to work with the immigrant families who

---

St. John Neumann

b. March 28, 1811

d. January 5, 1860

Founder of the Sisters of the Third Order of St. Francis

Feast Day — January 5

Meaning of name — God is gracious, from the Hebrew *yôhānān*

Latin		
Joannes	Johanna f.	Jonny
Johannes		Jack
	Norwegian	Jackson
French	Johannes	Jenkin
Jean		Sean
Jeannot	*Dutch*	Zane
Jeanne ⎤ f.	Jan	Jackie m., f.
Jeannette ⎦		Gianna
	Hungarian	Jan
Spanish	Janos	Jane
Juan		Janie
Juanna ⎤ f.	*Russian*	Janet
Juanita ⎦	Ivan	Janice
	Irish	Janis
Italian	Seán	Jean ⎤
Giovanni	Eoin	Jeannette
Giovanna f.		Jeanine
	Scottish	Joanna
Portuguese	Ian	Joanne
João		Johanna ⎟ f.
Jovanna f.	*Welsh*	Jonelle
	Evan	Shawn
German		Zaneta
Johannes	*English*	Juanita ⎦
Johann	John	
Hannes	Johnny	
Hans	Jon	

---

parents sent their son to Czechoslovakia's best schools, including the seminary at Budweis. Although John finished his seminary studies in 1835, he could not be ordained immediately.

He therefore wrote to Bishop John Dubois of the diocese of New York, which then covered all of New York state and part of New Jersey. John volunteered to work with the immigrant families who

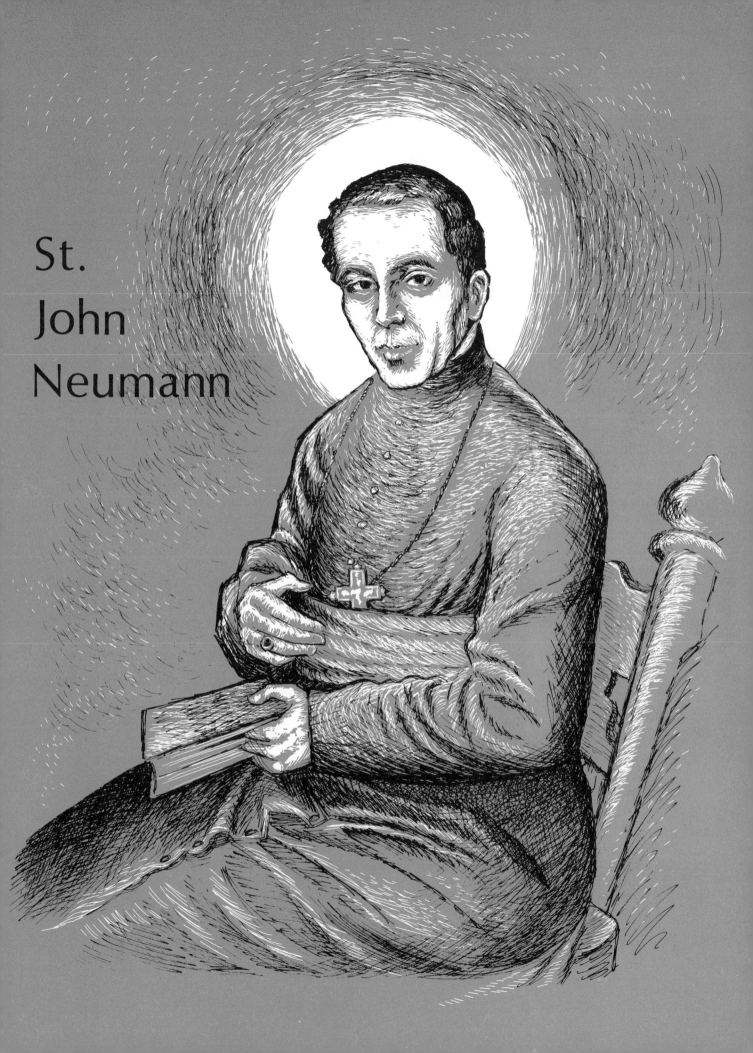

St.
John
Neumann

were settling that area of the growing United States. He was well prepared to help immigrants from almost every corner of Europe, since he knew six modern languages, including German. But John heard nothing from Bishop Dubois. Nevertheless, he decided to set sail for New York anyway, where he hoped to find a bishop to ordain him and to assign him priestly work.

Without saying good-bye to his parents except by letter, John sailed from France in April, 1836, and arrived in New York City a month later. In the meantime, Bishop Dubois had answered John's letter, telling him that he was anxious for his help. But the letter had not reached John because he was at sea.

Fortunately, John visited the bishop shortly after getting off the ship. Bishop Dubois was delighted to see him, since he needed another priest to serve the German parishes in the huge area between Albany and Buffalo in upstate New York. Bishop Dubois ordained John a priest on June 25 that same year. Soon after that the young Father Neumann was off to serve the upstate immigrant parishes, work which he would continue for the next four years.

John met many priests who were members of the Congregation of the Most Holy Redeemer. This Congregation of priests and brothers was founded in Italy in 1732 by St. Alphonsus Liguori. John decided to join their number, and thus in 1842 the Redemptorists, as they were commonly called, welcomed him. In fact, John was the first member to join the Congregation in the United States. From then on he wrote "C.SS.R." after his name, letters which in Latin are the initials of the Redemptorists.

John served in parishes in Baltimore and in Pittsburgh and in various positions as an administrator. John had a knack for handling details and for working well with people. For two years he was the head of all the Redemptorists in the country. He was especially concerned that parishes organize and build schools whenever possible.

In 1851 Bishop Francis Kenrick of Philadelphia, who had long recognized Father Neumann's leadership, was appointed the archbishop of Baltimore. Archbishop Kenrick recommended to Pope Pius IX that the new bishop of Philadelphia be John Neumann. The Pope accepted this advice and made that appointment. Thus, on March 28, 1852, Archbishop Kenrick ordained John as the fourth bishop of Philadelphia.

Bishop Neumann had only eight more years to live, but that was long enough for him to accomplish many important tasks. Over eighty churches were built in the diocese. The parish schools were organized into a diocese-wide system, and the enrollment increased from five hundred to nine thousand students. The Christian Brothers and several Orders of sisters came to teach in these schools. The sisters of the Third Order of St. Francis, founded by Bishop Neumann, worked in the Philadelphia Diocese. The bishop started a preparatory seminary for boys interested in the priesthood. Work was begun on the new Cathedral of Sts. Peter and Paul.

Bishop Neumann established the devotion to the Blessed Sacrament known as the Forty Hours throughout the diocese. He wrote dozens of articles for Catholic periodicals and newspapers, as well as two catechisms and a book of Bible stories, which were published in German. Most of the people in his diocese spoke and read German better than they did English. The "Little Bishop," as his people called him, since he was but 5 feet 4 inches tall, was never short on work. Bishop Neumann perhaps was the busiest bishop ever. He even found time each year to visit every parish and mission throughout his diocese. The people knew and loved him dearly.

Bishop Neumann was not quite fifty-one years old when he died in Philadelphia in 1860. His life of simple piety and hard work for the Church convinced many to press the authorities for his canonization. In 1921, Pope Benedict XV declared John Neumann a venerable. But not all the Church authorities agreed with Pope Benedict. Some argued that Neumann had not demonstrated great heroic virtue during his lifetime. But Pope Benedict told these critics that "even the most simple works, performed with constant perfection in the midst of inevitable difficulties, spell heroism in any servant of God." The Pope was convinced that Bishop Neumann had lived a most virtuous life.

Then, in 1963, Pope Paul VI proclaimed Venerable Neumann a blessed, and on June 19, 1977, the same Pope declared him a saint. Present in St. Peter's Square for the open-air ceremony were twenty thousand people. The happy crowd included two men and one woman who through John Neumann's intercession with God had been miraculously cured of medically untreatable injuries, bone cancer, and acute peritonitis. At the Mass, John Cardinal Krol, since 1961 the new saint's successor as the bishop of Philadelphia, joined Pope Paul at the altar.

That same day, back in the bishop-saint's diocese, at Aston, Pennsylvania, Archbishop Jean Jadot, then apostolic delegate to the United States, offered a special Mass at the motherhouse of the sisters of the Third Order of St. Francis. And in Philadelphia the churches were filled for special services, especially at the Neumann Shrine in St. Peter's Church. There the saint's body lies in a glass case under an altar.

ST

FRANCES   XAVIER

CABRINI

St. Frances Xavier Cabrini

Ever since she was a little girl, Maria Francesca Cabrini wanted to be a missionary to China, but her wish never came true. Instead God planned for Maria to establish a Congregation of sisters who would work for the Lord in many nations, including her home country of Italy, but not in China.

After graduating from school at age eighteen, Maria began a career she loved—working with children. She first taught in public schools. Next, at the request of the parish priest at Codogno, Italy, she took charge of an orphanage. For six years, with love and concern she cared for this house full of children who no longer had parents or whose parents could not take care of their needs. Maria was never busier or happier.

In 1877 Maria's bishop asked her to establish a religious Congregation of sisters who would care for and educate girls. Maria took that suggestion to heart and that year founded the Missionary Sisters of the Sacred Heart. Within two years the sisters opened schools not only in Codogno but also in two other cities. In 1887 the sisters started a children's home and school in Rome, Italy's bustling capital. The Cabrini sisters were both mother and teacher to hundreds of children. They cared for their every need, twenty-four hours a day. The sisters taught the girls religion, spelling, reading, arithmetic, geography, etc.; they played games with them; they cooked their meals; they sewed their clothes; they bandaged scraped knees.

In the late 1800s thousands of people said good-bye to Italy and other European countries and emigrated to the United States. There in the New World they hoped to rebuild their lives and live at greater peace and comfort than they found possible in the Old World. Since

---

St. Frances Xavier Cabrini

b. July 15, 1850

d. December 22, 1917

Founder of the Missionary Sisters of the Sacred Heart

First United States citizen to be canonized

Feast Day — November 13

Meaning of name — free, from the old German *franko*

Latin	*Norwegian*
Franciscus m.	Franciskus m.
Francisca	*German*
French	Franziska
Françoise	Franz m.
Francis ⟍ m.	*English*
François ⟋	Frances
Spanish, Portuguese	Frannie
Francisca	Francie
Francisco m.	Francine
Italian	Fanny
Francesca	Fran m., f.
Francesco ⟍ m.	Francis
Franco ⟋	Frank ⟍ m.

25

many of the immigrants stayed in New York City, they looked forward to having priests and sisters who spoke the European languages and who understood the Old World customs staff their parishes. It was Archbishop Michael Corrigan who wrote to Mother Cabrini, as she was called, and asked her to come to New York City with her sisters and work in the "Little Italy" of that city. Pope Leo XIII encouraged Mother Cabrini to do the same. He told her, "Go to the West, not to the East," since she still wanted to be a missionary to China.

In March, 1889, Mother Cabrini and six sisters arrived in New York City, worn out after a long and uncomfortable winter crossing of the Atlantic. To their surprise and disappointment, the archbishop was not quite ready for them. The sisters had to stay in a run-down hotel until the archbishop located a convent. But the sisters lost no time in getting to work. That same year they established an orphanage and a school for four hundred girls in Little Italy. A year later Mother Cabrini organized a novitiate or training center for Italian-American girls who wanted to join the Missionary Sisters of the Sacred Heart.

Despite frail health and the hardship of travel seventy-five years ago, Mother Cabrini made thirty crossings of the Atlantic by ship. She also rode thousands of miles by train, carriage, and even horseback to set up and then later visit convents, schools, orphanages, and hospitals of her missionary sisters. By 1909 Mother Cabrini's Congregation had one thousand sisters working in fifty foundations in eight countries—Italy, Spain, France, the United States, Costa Rica, Panama, Argentina, and Chile.

In the United States the Cabrini sisters worked in such cities as Seattle, Denver, New Orleans, Los Angeles, and New York. Besides caring for children, the sick, and the elderly, they regularly visited prisoners locked up in the jails of New York and Chicago. They even brought comfort to the condemned men on the Sing Sing Prison's death row.

Mother Cabrini was a smart businesswoman. She knew how to buy property, hire carpenters, plumbers, and bricklayers, talk with lawyers, and budget money for a project. Once, when Mother Cabrini felt that the dimensions of a building as told to her by a real estate agent were incorrect, she and her sisters late at night took tape measures and foot by foot on their hands and knees measured the outside of the building. Sure enough, the agent's figures were far from accurate. He had tried to cheat the sisters, but Mother Cabrini was a step ahead of him. Fortunately, most people who did business with the sisters were honest.

The sisters begged most of the money they needed to pay their bills and to care for the children, the sick, and the elderly under their charge. Most of the money was donated by immigrant families in the large cities. These families were almost always hard pressed for funds, but they often sacrificed nickels and dimes to help people even poorer than themselves.

Mother Cabrini loved her adopted country dearly. She knew the United States and its varied people very well, since in her work she traveled widely from coast to coast. One day in 1910 Mother Cabrini took the oath of citizenship in a Seattle courtroom. She was now a naturalized citizen of the United States. Today she ranks as the first American citizen to be named a saint of the Church.

During the last six years of her life, Mother Cabrini's health gradually worsened, but she continued a steady pace of work and travel. At her sisters' request, she never retired as their superior general. Three days before Christmas in 1917, at an Italian-American school in Chicago, where her sisters lived and worked, Mother Cabrini quietly died.

In 1946 Mother Cabrini was named a saint by Pope Pius XII. The saint's body rests in the chapel of the Mother Cabrini High School in New York City.

St. Frances Xavier Cabrini is the patron of emigrants, hospital administrators, and the foreign missions.

St. Martin de Porres

Over four hundred years ago sleek sailing ships loaded with a human cargo of slaves from Africa would dock almost daily at Callao near Lima, Peru. The slaves who had somehow survived that long voyage west across the Atlantic and around Cape Horn would then be hustled ashore. Indeed, many who were crowded into the ship's hold in Africa did not make it to the marketplace. They died because of disease, hunger, and mistreatment while at sea.

To the Spanish businessmen who watched the frightened blacks file ashore, the cargo was only merchandise to be bought, traded, and sold. But to a white-robed Dominican brother named Martin de Porres, who often was there at dockside, the slaves were God's special creatures, as were men and women everywhere.

St. Martin de Porres

b. December 9, 1579

d. November 4, 1639

Feast Day — formerly on November 5

Meaning of name — warlike, from the Latin *Mars, Martis*

Latin	*German*
Martinus	**Martin**
French	**Martina f.**
Martin	*Norwegian*
Martine f.	**Martin**
Spanish, Italian	**Marten**
Martino	*English*
Portuguese	**Martin**
Martinho	**Marty**
Dutch	**Martie f.**
Martijn	

Martin devoted his life to caring for the poor and the unfortunate of Lima. On frequent visits to Callao, Martin (who was half-black himself) would board the slave ships, crawl into the stinking holds, and bring whatever comforts he could to the neglected and terrified slaves. He would bandage open sores, cleanse wounds, speak kindly to them, offer fresh fruit. He would do his best to bring comfort to the suffering. If he was not at the slave ships, Martin was doing similar social work at the prisons of Lima and in the ghettos where the poor lived in deplorable conditions. He would bring families blankets, clothes, bread and fruit, medicine, candles, money for a bride's dowry, whatever Martin might have that day to help them.

In the sixteenth century the Spanish officials in Peru did little to ease the suffering of the poor. No government welfare system supplied food stamps, low-rent housing, clothing, and medicine to people who could not support themselves. Peru was a nation of a wealthy ruling class from Spain and poor Indians who were native to that country. Thousands of slaves from Africa, along with the Indians, supplied the work force.

Martin himself was a half-caste. His father, Juan de Porres, a Spanish knight, had not married Martin's mother, a freed black woman from Panama named Anna Velasquez. The record of Martin's baptism read, "Martin, son of an unknown father." But when Martin was eight years old his father agreed to let his mulatto-skinned son take his last name, and Señor Porres paid for Martin's education. For two years Martin attended classes in Guayaquil, Ecuador, the neighboring country to the west of Peru, where his father worked.

When Martin was twelve years old, he was apprenticed to a *cirujano* in Lima, a man who was a barber as well as a druggist, doctor, and surgeon. From this teacher Martin learned how to cut hair and give a shave, mix herbs to form medicines, treat colds and coughs, and set broken bones. In his spare time away from the *cirujano's* clinic, Martin practiced these skills in the ghetto, where he treated the poor who could not afford to visit a clinic or a hospital.

When Martin made his rounds in the ghetto, he often met Dominican priests, brothers, and sisters of the friaries and convents in Lima. These Dominicans, along with other religious and lay people, such as Rose de Flores (St. Rose of Lima), gave of their time, talent, and money to look after the poor.

Martin decided to join that Order. When he was fifteen years old, he joined the friary of the Most Holy Rosary in Lima, where he worked and lived as a lay brother. In his humility Martin never thought that it would be possible for the Dominicans to accept him as a full-fledged religious brother. But as time moved on his superiors could not help but notice the rigorous schedule of prayer and service that Martin followed. Nine years later they asked Martin to join the Dominicans as a religious brother.

Martin's job at the friary was to care for the sick and the elderly priests and brothers. He handled his duties as infirmarian most ably because his first concern was caring for people and because he was well trained as a *cirujano*. Martin also had charge each day of

taking bread, fruit, other foods, and whatever money the friary could spare to poor families in the ghetto. Eventually, Martin helped establish an orphanage and a hospital to care for foundlings, babies whose parents abandoned them, usually because they were too poor to feed, clothe, and shelter them.

Martin even looked after the abandoned animals of Lima. If he found a stray dog or cat, he would take the lonesome animal to his sister's home for a bone or a saucer of milk. Martin could not even be harsh with mice, who, he said, only bothered people because they were hungry. Everyone gets hungry. Martin's heart was in the right place.

Martin's reputation as a holy and humble Dominican brother and as a humanitarian became known far beyond Lima. When the archbishop of Mexico City visited Lima in 1639 and became seriously sick, he asked that Brother Martin nurse him and pray with him. Shortly after Martin's visit, the archbishop recovered. Martin's superiors had granted him permission, at the archbishop's request, to travel to Mexico City and work for the archbishop. But Martin never made that journey since he died in November that year.

As Martin lay on his deathbed, the Spanish viceroy, the Count of Chinchón, who was the king's chief officer in Peru, visited Martin. He knelt by his bed and asked for Martin's blessing. The "Father of Charity," the "Father of the Poor," as Brother Martin was known in Peru, was loved by both the rich and the poor.

Because of his humility, holiness, and love of all creatures, Martin's fellow Dominicans judged him to be a saint long before he died. Many of the priests and brothers asked him to direct their spiritual lives, since they knew that Martin was close to God. Martin helped his Dominican brothers and all whom he met in Lima and Callao to find peace of soul as well as strength of body.

Sometimes the official procedure of naming a saint of the Church takes centuries. It was not until 1837 that Pope Gregory XVI declared Martin a blessed, and it was another 125 years until he was proclaimed a saint. In

ST.
MARTIN
DE
PORRES

1962 Pope John XXIII, the Holy Father who visited the prisons and the poor of Rome, canonized Blessed Martin a saint.

The "Saint of Universal Brotherhood," Martin saw Jesus in every person he met, whether that individual was a slave from Africa, an archbishop from Mexico City, a viceroy from Spain, the sick-poor of Lima, or the Dominicans of the Holy Rosary Friary. The patron of interracial justice, Martin de Porres knew and practiced the belief that no one should ever be denied equality because of religion, skin color, or position in society.

St. Martin is also the patron of hairdressers.

2. New Testament Saints

Sts. Joachim and Anne

Over two thousand years ago a Jewish couple named Joachim and Anne kept hoping and praying that a baby would be born to them. More than anything else they wanted a boy or a girl they could love and teach, a baby they could share their lives with. Their home in Israel was too quiet, too neat, and too lonely—no children's laughter, no toys cluttering the living room floor, no helpers for the housework, no one to take visiting the neighbors on weekend afternoons.

But when God saw that the time was right, he blessed Joachim and Anne with a baby girl. They named her Mary. This baby grew up to be the Mother of Jesus.

These events about the birth of Mary are not described in the Bible, which says nothing about Mary's parents. But information handed down by the early Christians from one generation to the next gave us this story. About the year 170 this information about Joachim and Anne was written down, and thus we know it today. Other ac-

---

Sts. Joachim and Anne

Last century before Jesus

Parents of Mary, the Blessed Mother

Feast Day — July 26

Meaning of name — grace (Anne), from the Hebrew *hannāh*

—the Lord will judge (Joachim), from the Hebrew *yōyāqīm*

Latin	English	French, German, Dutch, English
Anna	Anne	
	Ann	Joachim
French	Annette	
Anne	Anita	*Spanish*
Annette	Anna	Joaquim
	Chana	Joaquin
Spanish	Chanah	
Ana	Dina	*Italian*
Anita	Hannah	Joachimo
	Hanita	Joachino
Italian	Nan	
Anna	Nance	
	Nancy	
German	Nanette	
Anna	Nanine	
Annie	Nanny	
Ännchen	Nina	
	Ninon	
Norwegian		
Anna		

---

counts say that Mary's father was named Heli, Cleopas, Eliacim, Jonachir, or Sadoc. He was said to be a prosperous sheep owner.

As early as the year 550, churches were named in honor of the grandparents of Jesus. St. Anne's Church in Jerusalem is reported to be the site of the birthplace of Mary. Some say that Mary was born close to an entrance to the old city of Jerusalem called the Gate of the Lady Mary.

Paintings tell us how the Christians of centuries ago remembered Joachim and Anne. About the year 800, for example, Pope Leo III presented a vestment which was decorated with paintings of Joachim, Anne, and Mary to a famous church in Rome called St. Mary

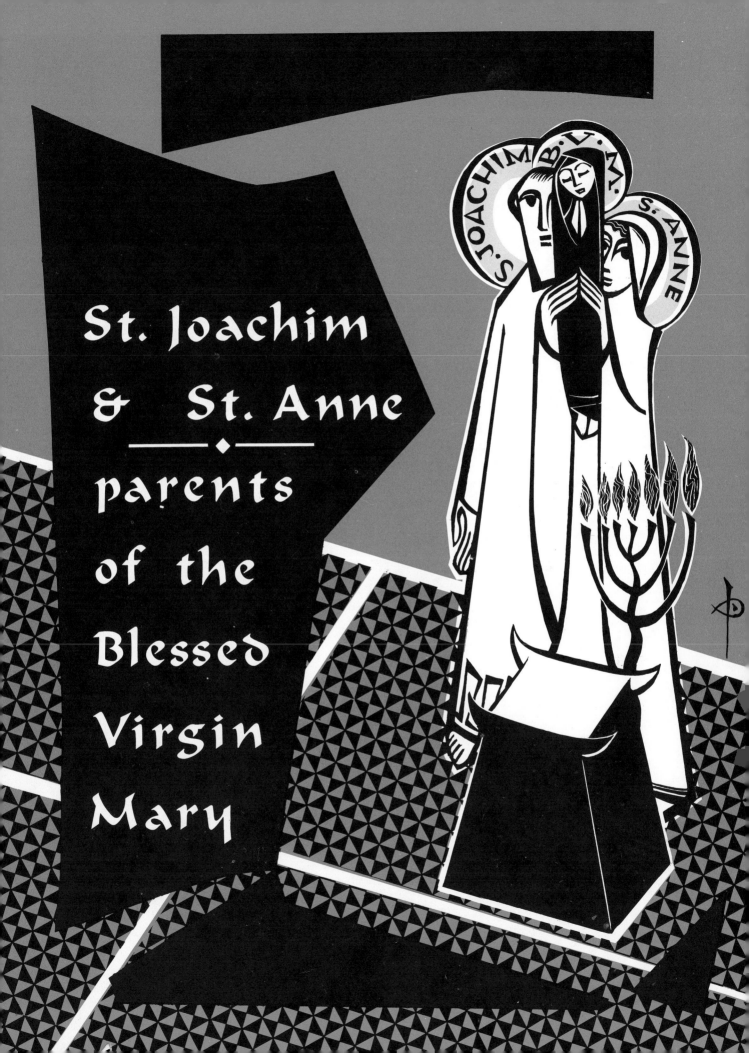

St. Joachim & St. Anne
———— • ————
parents of the Blessed Virgin Mary

Major. Joachim is often pictured holding his daughter in his arms. He is also portrayed bringing two doves to the Temple in Jerusalem, the main place of worship for the Jewish people. There the doves would be offered in thanksgiving to God for the birth of Mary. Artists have painted Anne teaching Mary to read the Bible or walking hand-in-hand with her. Sometimes Anne is pictured with Jesus and Mary.

The French people, both in France and in Quebec, Canada, have a special devotion to St. Anne—and to St. Joachim, too. Pilgrims travel long distances and at considerable expense to visit and to pray in magnificent churches dedicated to St. Anne at Auray, which is in Brittany in western France, and at Beaupré, which is near Quebec City. Many miracles have occurred at these shrines.

As with most of the early saints, nothing for certain is known about the death and burial of Joachim and Anne. The Greeks claim, however, that the relics of St. Anne were brought from Bethlehem in the Holy Land to Constantinople, now Istanbul, in

Turkey during the year 710. But the French say that two hundred years earlier St. Auspicius brought St. Anne's body to the city of Apt in their country.

St. Anne, whose name means "grace," is the patron of twenty or more causes, places, and professions. She is not only the patron of Apt, Brittany, Florence, Naples, Innsbruck, and French Canada, but also, to name a few, of mothers and grandmothers, women who are looking for husbands, housewives, the imprisoned, weavers, stocking-makers, lace-makers, cabinet-makers, broom-makers, stablemen, goldsmiths, old-clothes dealers, fishermen, the blind, the deaf, and the mute. People also ask St. Anne's intercession for protection from bad weather and to find lost objects.

The celebration of Mother's Day is also associated with St. Anne. Years ago on "Mothering Sunday," in honor of St. Anne, children would go "a-mothering" and bring flowers, gifts, cakes, and cookies to their mothers.

St. Mary

There's probably not a Catholic church on earth without an altar or a picture dedicated to Mary. Each day countless Hail Marys are prayed by men and women, boys and girls, asking Mary, the Blessed Mother, for help. She is "our sure way to Christ," said Pope St. Pius X. Hundreds of shrines, ranging from tiny roadside chapels to magnificent cathedrals, speak of her greatness.

Among Mary's titles are "Our Lady of the Rosary," "Our Lady of Guadalupe," "Our Lady of the Snows," even "Our Lady of the Earthquake" and "Our Lady of the Pine Tree." From the first moment of her life, Mary lived without a trace of sin. She is the only saint who both in body and soul is in heaven. The queen of all saints is Mary, the Blessed Virgin, the Mother of God.

When she was growing up in Israel, Mary did not know that she would become the Mother of God. When she was about fourteen years old, God sent the Archangel Gabriel to give Mary a very important message. He told her that she was to be the Mother of Jesus. "Rejoice, O highly favored daughter! The Lord is with you. Blessed are you among women," announced the angel. Mary at first was puzzled by that message. Then Gabriel said: "Do not fear, Mary. You have found favor with God. You shall conceive and bear a son and give him the name of Jesus" (Luke 1:28-31).

Mary answered Gabriel: "I am the servant of the Lord." What a

---

St. Mary

First century

Mother of God, Mother of the Church

Major Feast Days — January 1
August 15
September 8
December 8

Meaning of name — Miriam (sister of Moses), from the Hebrew *miryām*

Latin	*Welsh*	Marian
Maria	Mair	Marion
French	*Irish*	Marianne
		Mariella
Marie	Maire	Marietta
Manette	Maureen	Mariette
Manon	Maura	Marice
Marianne	Moira	Maris
Mariette	Moya	Marisa
Marion	*German*	Marina
Mimi		Marla
Maryse	Marie	Mercy
Spanish	Maria	Merry
María	*(Austrian)*	Mimi
Marita	Mitzi	Minnie
Marquita	*English*	Miriam
Italian	Mary	Mitzi
Maria	Marie	Myrtle
Mariana	Maria	Maura
Portuguese	Mae	Maurella
Maria	May	Marilyn
Polish	Mame	Moll
Marya	Mamie	Molly
Norwegian	Mayme	Poll
Maria	Marella	Polly
	Marilla	Alma
	Mariam	Rosemary

powerful message! What an exciting moment for Mary and for the world!

Little is known about Mary's early life. Tradition tells us that she was the daughter of holy parents named Joachim and Anne (*see* p. 32) and that she was a distant relative of the great Jewish leader King David, who ruled the Holy Land centuries before Mary was born. When Mary was a little girl, perhaps about three years old, her parents brought her to the Temple in Jerusalem. There Mary lived with other children. Prior to the angel's visit, Mary was engaged to marry Joseph, a carpenter, who cared for her and later for Jesus.

With Joseph, Mary traveled the many miles from Nazareth to Bethlehem to register their names in the city of David where their ancestors had been born. The Roman officials had ordered that a census be taken to count all the people in the land of Israel that year. Bethlehem that winter was so crowded with visitors that Mary and Joseph could not find a hotel room. The only lodging available was a stable just outside town. That night, as shepherds watched their flocks nearby, Mary gave birth to Jesus.

Some months before the first Christmas, Mary had visited her kinswoman Elizabeth, who was also expecting a baby. That baby was John the Baptist. A few days after Jesus' birth, Mary and Joseph brought Jesus to the Temple to be presented to God by the priests. Twelve years later a worried Mary and Joseph found Jesus in that Temple, where he was talking to the rabbis or teachers. For three long days Mary and Joseph had searched for Jesus, who had been separated from them in that huge city of Jerusalem. From that event until the public life of Jesus that began when he was about thirty years old, the Gospels tell us little about Mary, Joseph, and Jesus. We know only that the Holy Family returned to Nazareth where Jesus "grew and became strong; he was full of wisdom, and God's blessings were upon him" (Luke 2:40).

During Jesus' public life Mary is mentioned as being at the wedding celebration at Cana. In fact, it was Mary who asked Jesus to change the water into wine so that the bride and groom would have enough wine to serve their guests. That was Jesus' first miracle. On the first Good Friday, Mary was also on Mount Calvary, where she waited and suffered quietly under the cross as Jesus was dying. And Mary was with the apostles in the Upper Room. There on that first Pentecost Day, the Holy Spirit gave them the strength to preach Jesus' teachings far and wide. Mary, the Blessed Virgin, the Mother of God, is also the Mother of the Church.

Mary lived for some years after that Pentecost in Jerusalem or, it is thought, in Ephesus in Asia Minor, where St. John the Apostle preached. (Just before he died on the cross, Jesus asked John to take care of his Mother.) At the end of her life, Mary was taken to heaven, both body and soul. In 1950, Pope Pius XII, in an elaborate ceremony in St. Peter's Square at the Vatican, proclaimed to the world that "the Immaculate Mother of God was assumed body and soul to heavenly glory." The holy day of the Assumption of Mary on August 15 celebrates this event.

On December 8, the holy day honoring Mary's Immaculate Conception, the Church celebrates its belief that Mary was conceived without sin. In 1854 Pope Pius IX proclaimed that message to the world. Since 1846, under the title of the Immaculate Conception, Mary has been the patron of the United States. Immaculate Mary, the Mother of God, the Mother of the Church, with loving concern gives her children encouragement and understanding.

The calendar lists many feast days for Mary, more than for any other saint. January 1 celebrates Mary as the Mother of God. New Year's Day is thus Mary's Mother's Day. A month later on February 2 the Church remembers the occasion that Mary and Jesus received a special blessing in the Temple. May 31 is the feast of the Visitation of Mary to Elizabeth; August 15, the Assumption of Mary to heaven; August 22, the Queenship of Mary. September 8 is Mary's birthday. September 15 honors Mary as Our Lady of Sorrows, remembering the suffering which she endured. October 7 is the feast of Mary,

Our Lady of the Rosary

Our Lady of the Rosary. Other feast days honor Mary, too.

Through the centuries the Blessed Mother has appeared many times in person to boys and girls, men and women (some of these apparitions are described below). On these occasions Mary's message to these people, and to the whole world, was to lead good lives, to pray daily, especially for peace. Today magnificent churches stand on the spots where Mary appeared. Pilgrims travel from near and far to pray at these shrines and perhaps to be cured of a sickness or to have a favor granted through Mary's intercession with God.

In 1830 Mary appeared three times to St. Catherine Labouré in the chapel of the Sisters of Charity motherhouse in Paris, France. The Blessed Mother directed Catherine to arrange to make a medal bearing an image of Mary as the Immaculate Conception and to encourage that particular devotion to Mary. That medal, commonly called the Miraculous Medal since 1832 when it was first crafted, is worn today by millions.

In 1858, at Lourdes, France, the Blessed Mother appeared eighteen times to fourteen-year-old Bernadette Soubirous. On one of her visits, Mary told St. Bernadette, "I am the Immaculate Conception."

In 1879, at Knock in western Ireland, Mary appeared to about twenty members of the parish church in that village. In 1917, in Fatima, Portugal, Mary appeared in several consecutive months, always on the thirteenth, to three shepherd children: Lúcia and her cousins Jacinta and Francisco, ages ten, seven, and eight. Mary told the children to remind the world to pray the Rosary, to pray for peace. In 1967 Pope Paul VI and in 1982 Pope John Paul II were among the pilgrims to visit Mary's shrine at Fatima. The Holy Fathers also visited Lúcia, a sister in a convent, the only one of the three children living at that time.

Years earlier, in 1531, near Mexico City, Mexico, the Blessed Mother visited a poor peasant named Juan Diego. When Bishop Zumárraga of that city refused to believe that Mary had appeared to Juan Diego, the poor

man, following the bishop's bidding, asked the Virgin at her next visit for a sign to take to the bishop. Mary then directed Juan Diego to climb a mountain, where at the top he would find some flowers. There on Tepeyac Mountain, where scarcely anything grew in the summer, let alone in December, Juan Diego found many roses. He returned to Mary and she arranged them in his *tilma* or coat. Juan hurried to Bishop Zumárraga. When Juan opened his *tilma,* the flowers dropped to the floor. To his amazement the bishop saw not only the roses but also on the *tilma* the image of the Virgin in beautiful colors, a second sign of her appearance to Juan Diego.

Today pilgrims come, as they have for four centuries, to the shrine of Our Lady of Guadalupe at Tepeyac. Juan Diego's *tilma* is preserved in that basilica. In 1979 one of the pilgrims was Pope John Paul II. That year the smiling Pope visited Mary's shrines at Knock, Ireland, and at Czestochowa, Poland. In 1945 Pope Pius XII named Mary, Our Lady of Guadalupe, as the patron of the Americas. In 1910 Pope St. Pius X had named her the "Mother of Latin America." The feast day of Our Lady of Guadalupe is December 12.

The Church remembers Mary in a variety of services, prayers, and customs. In the Litany of Loreto, Mary is addressed by many titles, including those of "Mystical Rose," "Tower of David," and "Seat of Wisdom." The Hail Mary is second only to the Our Father as the most familiar prayer of the Church. It is the Hail Mary that is prayed over and over again in the Rosary. "Pray for us, O holy Mother of God," we say. Each Saturday is dedicated to Mary. May and October are months of special devotion to Mary —processions, parades, rallies, prayer services. Orders of priests, brothers, and sisters, such as the Oblates of Mary Immaculate, the Marists, the Claretians, and the Humility of Mary, dedicate their work to the Blessed Virgin. Lay persons through the Legion of Mary do the same.

People wear medals which bear the Virgin's image. Many carry rosaries in their purses or pockets. Millions of Christians are baptized Mary, Maria, or some other form of the Virgin's name. Thousands of schools, churches, hospitals, and other structures are dedicated to Mary. Among them is the world-famous Notre Dame Cathedral in Paris, France. Similarly named is the University of Notre Dame in Indiana. States, ships, planes, even wines, are named after Mary. The National Shrine of the Immaculate Conception in Washington, D.C., is dedicated to St. Mary, the Immaculate Conception and the patron of the United States. With such variety the Church and the people of God remember and love St. Mary, the Blessed Virgin, the Mother of God.

St. Joseph

In nations from one end of the globe to the other, schools, churches, altars, religious Orders, hospitals, and cities and towns, both large and small, are named after St. Joseph. His is a common name given to children at baptism and confirmation. Joseph lived over two thousand years ago, a descendant of the royal family of King David of Israel. The Bible tells us that he was a "just man," meaning a good man. This man of God became the husband of Mary, the Mother of God, and the foster father of Jesus, the Savior of the world.

It wasn't always easy for Joseph, though he was a patient and just man, to do what God asked him to do. When an angel told Joseph that Mary would be the Mother of Jesus and that he should take Mary as his wife, he did so immediately. Since Mary would soon give birth, the four-day journey from Nazareth in Galilee to Bethlehem in Judea was especially difficult. But the Roman law required Joseph to register his name with the census officials in Bethlehem, the city of his birth.

In Bethlehem, Joseph had to be satisfied with a stable for cattle and sheep rather than a cozy room in a hotel as the place for Jesus to be born. The city was crowded with visitors that winter; he had no other choice. Nor was it easy for Joseph to obey the angel's order to get up in the middle of the night and to flee with his

St. Joseph

First century
Foster father of Jesus
Husband of Mary

Feast Days — March 19
May 1

Meaning of name — He shall add.,
    from the Hebrew *yôsêph*

Latin	
Josephus	**Josep**
	Yusup
French	
Josèphe	*German*
Josephine f.	**Josef**
	Sepp
Spanish	**Josefa f.**
José	
Pepe	*(Austrian)*
Pepito	**Peppi**
Josefina f.	
Pepita	*Norwegian*
	Josef
Italian	
Giuseppe	*Russian*
Beppo	**Iosif**
Peppo	
Giuseppina f.	*Arabic Languages*
	Yussuf
Portuguese	
	English
José	**Joseph**
Pepe	**Joe**
Pepito	**Jo m., f.**
Josephina f.	**Jocile**
	Joselin
Hungarian	**Joselyn f.**
Jozef	**Josephine**
Jozefa f.	**Josepha**
	Josette
Slavic Languages	**Jozy**
Josip	**Pheny**
Joska	**Fifi**
Josko	

41

family to Egypt. King Herod planned to hunt down and kill the newborn Savior.

Again, some time later, after King Herod had died and the danger had passed, an angel told Joseph to return home. Joseph did so, bringing his family to Nazareth, where tradition tells us he earned his living as a carpenter.

The Bible does not tell us many other facts about Joseph. We do know, however, that he was present at the Temple in Jerusalem for ceremonies with Jesus and Mary shortly after the Savior's birth. And we know that twelve years later Joseph and Mary spent three anxious days searching for Jesus, who had remained in Jerusalem after the celebration of the great Jewish feast of the Passover, talking with the teachers in the Temple. His parents did not completely understand Jesus' explanations to them that he had stayed in the city to be in his "Father's house" (Luke 2:49). Joseph and Mary were simply worried that their son was lost. After that event, the Bible reports nothing about Joseph, other than to mention that Jesus returned to Nazareth and was subject to his parents.

In Jewish society the sons in a family often learn their father's trade. We may assume that Joseph taught Jesus the skills of working with wood as a carpenter. Artists have often pictured Jesus helping Joseph with a project in his shop, handing him tools or steadying a board that Joseph was sawing. The Bible does not tell us when Joseph died, but it seems that he died before Jesus was thirty. There is no mention of Joseph being with Mary or Jesus during our Lord's last three years on earth, a time called Jesus' public life. Joseph no doubt was younger than fifty when he died. He probably married Mary before he was twenty, the usual age for a man in Palestine to marry in those days.

Artists have pictured Joseph holding the child Jesus, just as any father would frequently hold his child. Sometimes Joseph is carrying a green staff that has a flower blossoming from it. The flower is a sign of Joseph's selection by God to be the guardian of the Savior. Other artists have painted Joseph holding a lily. This white flower sym-

bolizes his goodness. Frequently, too, the Holy Family is pictured together, a customary event in a family.

Two feast days commemorate St. Joseph. March 19 is the more important of the two. The Church that day honors God's selection of Joseph as the husband of Mary and the protector of Jesus. The second feast, that of St. Joseph the Worker, is celebrated on May 1. Masses offered that day, as well as on Labor Day in September in the United States and Canada, emphasize how necessary and wholesome it is for people to work hard at their jobs as did St. Joseph. The Church chose May 1 to counteract the celebration in Communist countries, especially in Russia, of May Day. The Communists on that day celebrate the importance of work, but they do not point to St. Joseph as the patron of workers. St. Joseph is also remembered on the feast of the Holy Family, which is celebrated on the Sunday after Christmas.

Besides being the patron saint of all workers, St. Joseph is the patron of many other causes or peoples. He is the patron of families, of virgins, and of the sick and the dying. People pray to St. Joseph for a happy death, that is, to die at peace with God and with their family and friends, as did St. Joseph who died comforted by Mary and Jesus. St. Joseph is also the patron of prayer, the poor, those in authority, refugees, fathers, priests and religious, travelers, and because of his closeness to the Blessed Mother, he is the patron of devotion to Mary.

For as long as four hundred years, St. Joseph has been designated as the official patron of several nations: Mexico (1555), Canada (1624), Bohemia or western Czechoslovakia (1655), the Chinese missions (1678), and Belgium (1689). Perhaps in no place else is the memory of St. Joseph more honored than at the shrine of St. Joseph's Oratory in Montreal, Quebec. There a holy man named Brother André, who was declared a blessed by Pope John Paul II in 1982, established a special devotion to St. Joseph. Each year thousands of travelers from near and distant lands visit St. Joseph's Oratory.

In 1870 Pope Pius IX honored Joseph by naming him the patron of Catholics across the world. More recently other popes have called upon St. Joseph to give special help to certain causes. In 1937 Pope Pius XI chose him as the patron of the campaign against Communism. Then, in 1961, Pope John XXIII proclaimed Joseph as the heavenly protector of the Second Vatican Council, which called the bishops of the world to Rome to consider changes in the organization and the worship of the Church. That same Pope a year later ordered that St. Joseph's name be mentioned in the Eucharistic Prayer at Mass.

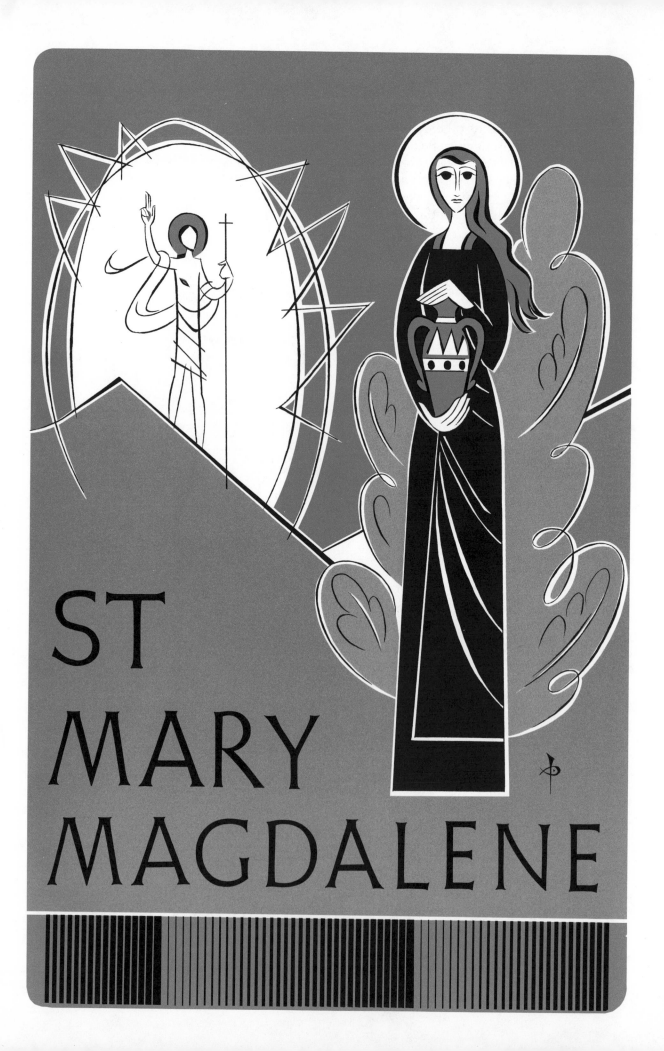

ST
MARY
MAGDALENE

St. Mary Magdalene

Easter Sunday is the most special Sunday of the year. Church bells ring long and joyously. Trumpets and trombones, organs and guitars join choirs and congregations in announcing that "Jesus has risen." White lilies and yellow jonquils decorate altars. The Easter candle burns in the sanctuary. The priest wears white vestments. The parishioners are often dressed in their best clothes, perhaps new for that special day.

On Easter morning the priest reads the account of Jesus' resurrection from the dead. "Do not be frightened," the angel said to the women at the tomb. "I know you are looking for Jesus the crucified, but he is not here. He has been raised, exactly as he promised. Come and see the place where he was laid" (Matthew 28:5-6). It is great news. Jesus is risen, alleluia!

On that first Easter Sunday almost two thousand years ago, Mary Magdalene was the first person to see the risen Savior. Mary and other women had come to the tomb just before dawn that morning in order to put sweet-smelling ointment on Jesus' body. They were wondering who would help them move the huge stone that was in front of the tomb, which was in a garden. But to their surprise when they arrived at the tomb, two angels dressed in bright, shining clothes told them the marvelous message, "He is not here. He has been raised."

Soon Peter and another apostle met the holy women. Mary told them, "The Lord has been taken from the tomb! We don't know where they have put him!" (John 20:2).

St. Mary Magdalene

First century

Feast Day — July 22

Meaning of name — of Magdala, from the Greek *magdalēnē*

French
Madeleine
Madelon
Magdelaine

Spanish
Madelena
Magdalena

Italian
Maddalena

Portuguese, Norwegian
Magdalena

German
Magdalena
Magda

English
Magdalene
Magdalen
Mada
Madge
Maidel
Marlene
Maud
Maun
Lena

The apostles looked at the empty tomb and then went home. They were confused since they did not know what Mary's message meant. Mary, too, was worried and remained in the garden wondering what to do next. Shortly, someone spoke to her, "Woman, why are you weeping? Who is it you are looking for?" (John 20:15).

Thinking that the voice was that of the gardener, Mary said, "Sir, if you are the one who carried him off, tell me where you have laid him and I will take him away" (John 20:15).

Then the speaker called her by name. "Mary," he said. When she turned she recognized Jesus. He told her to go and tell the apostles, who were in hiding, whom she had seen.

The Gospels say little else about Mary Magdalene. We do know that Jesus had cured her of a terrible affliction, being possessed by demons. Her last name tells us that she grew up near the fishing village of Magdala on the western shore of the Sea of Galilee. Mary was one of the women who often listened to Jesus as he preached to the people and worked miracles among them in Palestine.

Once Jesus was at a dinner at the home of a rich man named Simon. He was wealthy but he was not very polite, at least not that day. He did not offer Jesus water and a towel to wash and dry his feet. It was customary for a host to offer that service to a guest in that hot and dusty climate. But, during the dinner a woman who was known in the community as being very sinful came to Simon's house and washed Jesus' feet with her tears. She was crying bitterly because she was sorry for her sins. With her long hair she wiped her tears that fell on Jesus' feet, and then she put some expensive perfume on them. Jesus recognized that the woman was truly sorry for her sins and told her that they were forgiven. The rich man Simon was embarrassed. Though the name of this repentant woman is not given in the Gospels, she is often associated with Mary Magdalene, who is mentioned shortly after this event in St. Luke's Gospel.

Frequently artists picture Mary Magdalene carrying a jar and with her hair flowing freely about her. She is the patron of perfumers, tanners, glove-makers, and repentant people.

How Mary Magdalene spent her later years is not certain. One story tells how she went to Ephesus in Asia Minor with the Blessed Mother and St. John the Apostle. There, it is said, she died and was buried. In the year 811, Emperor Leo VI brought her relics to the Monastery of St. Lazarus in Constantinople. Another story suggests that she traveled to southern France and settled in Marseilles.

St. Martha

Centuries ago when Jesus was preaching in Palestine, two sisters named Mary and Martha and their brother Lazarus lived in Bethany, a village a couple of miles from the busy capital city of Jerusalem. Now and then Jesus would take a break from his work and visit this family. They were good friends. Jesus enjoyed their company and they his.

Martha's reputation as an excellent cook was known throughout the neighborhood. If she was not just taking a cake from the oven, she was adding spices to a stew that simmered on the stove. She liked nothing better than to bustle about the kitchen, preparing snacks and meals for her brother and sister and their guests. It pleased Martha immensely that Jesus would visit their home. It was not every family in Bethany who could tell the neighbors that the famous preacher and miracle worker from Nazareth in Galilee had stopped by for dinner.

St. Martha

First century

Feast Day — July 29

Meaning of name — lady, from the Aramaic *mârthâ*

French
Marthe

Spanish, Italian
Marta

Portuguese, Norwegian
Martha

German
Martha
Marthe

English
Martha
Mart
Marty
Mat
Matty
Pat
Patty

Mary was the quiet type. She helped her sister with the housework, to be sure, but she preferred to be the hostess, to visit with the guests, to make them feel at home. When Jesus came she liked to listen to him talk about life here and hereafter, about his Father in heaven. During one particular visit Mary was so intent on listening to Jesus that she forgot to help Martha set the table and serve the supper. That bothered Martha a little and she scolded Jesus, "Lord, are you not concerned that my sister has left me to do the household tasks all alone? Tell her to help me" (Luke 10:40).

Jesus answered her, "Martha, Martha, you are anxious and upset about many things; one thing only is required. Mary has chosen the better portion and she shall not be deprived of it."

Jesus did not mean to offend Martha. He only wanted her to realize that by listening to him Mary was learning about God and the

SAINT MARTHA

kingdom of heaven. It was important too for Martha to be getting the supper on the table, since they were all hungry. But it was important for Mary—as it is for all of us—to take time to listen to the Lord.

On another occasion Jesus visited his friends and found the two sisters very sad. Lazarus had died just four days earlier. When Martha heard that Jesus was walking toward their village, she went down the street to meet him. She said to Jesus, "Lord, if you had been here, my brother would never have died" (John 11:21). Jesus assured the sad Martha that Lazarus would rise again. But Martha thought that Jesus was talking only about the end of the world, when all the dead will rise again. She told him that she understood that and realized that Jesus was the Son of God. What a marvelous expression of faith Martha made that day!

Then Martha called Mary, who was grieving inside their house, and told her that Jesus had just reached Bethany. Hearing that news Mary rushed to Jesus with the same greeting that Martha had given him. "Lord, if you had been here, my brother would never have died." Jesus then asked the sisters to take him to Lazarus' tomb in the cemetery. There Jesus called forth their brother from the dead. It was one of Jesus' most remembered miracles.

Like sisters in just about every family, Martha and Mary had contrasting personalities. Martha was outgoing, energetic, and outspoken. Mary was quiet, reserved, the thinking type. Both sisters, each in a different way, realized that Jesus was the Son of God, the Savior of the world.

St. Martha is the patron of cooks, dieticians, and innkeepers.

Sts. Michael, Gabriel, and Raphael

Across the world, but especially in the Americas and Europe, thousands of boys answer to the name Michael and many others to Gabriel and Raphael. The original owners of these names never lived on earth like the other saints. Heaven has always been their home.

These saints, as angels, are spirits; that is, they do not have bodies. They have always enjoyed God's presence in heaven. Occasionally, however, an angel visits the earth as a messenger from God.

In heaven nine choirs of angels sing praise to God. Pope St. Gregory the Great listed the choirs as the cherubim, seraphim, thrones, dominations, principalities, powers, virtues, archangels, and angels.

The Bible mentions only three angels by name: the Archangels Michael, Gabriel, and Raphael. They and four other archangels stand before God's throne. Tradition tells us that the other four are Uriel, Raguel, Sariel, and Jerahmeel.

The most famous of all the angels is Michael. The Archangel Gabriel called him "one of the chief princes" of the angels (Daniel 10:13). Indeed, Michael has an important position in heaven. God has given him many responsibilities. The Archangel Michael is best known as the "captain of the heavenly host," the army of

---

Sts. Michael, Gabriel, and Raphael

Archangels

Feast Day — September 29

Meaning of names — Who is like God?
(Michael), from the Hebrew *mikhā'el*
— hero of God
(Gabriel), from the Hebrew *gabhri'ēl*
— God has healed.
(Raphael), from the Hebrew *rĕphā'ēl*

French	*Norwegian*
Michel	Michael
Michelle f.	Gabriel
Gabriel	Raphael
Gabrielle f.	*English*
Raphaël	Michael
Spanish	Mick
Miguel	Mickey
Gabriel	Miles
Rafael	Myles
Italian	Mike
Michele	Mitchel
Gabriello	Mitchell
Raffaello	Mitch
Raffaele	Midge ⟩ f.
Portuguese	Mia
Miguel	Gabriel
Gabriel	Gabby
German	Gabe
Michael	Gabi ⟩ m., f.
Gabriel	Gavi
Gabriela f.	Gabriela ⟩
Raffael	Gabriella ⟩ f.
Raffaela f.	Gabrielle ⟩
(Austrian)	Raphael
Raffel	Raff
Russian	Rafe
Mikhail	Raphaela f.
Misha	

---

good angels that fought the evil angels who would not obey God. Michael and his army forced these evil angels, who became known as demons or devils, out of heaven to the underworld called hell. Since then, Satan, the leader of the devils, has been trying to get even with God and Michael.

In Hebrew, Michael's name asks the question: Who is like God? Satan and his devils thought that they were as great as God, but Michael knew that this could not be. If an angel said that he was like to God, Michael routed him out of heaven.

Satan tries to this day to get even with God by bringing us temptations to sin, to do wrongful acts. But Michael works to rescue people from the power of Satan, especially at the hour of death. A famous prayer asks Michael to be "our safeguard against the wickedness and snares of the devil." Michael is asked to "defend us in battle," that is, the battle with the devil, the battle to live a good life. The reward for leading a good life is seeing God in heaven.

Tradition tells us that when a person dies, the Archangel Michael will lead that person's soul to judgment. And at the judgment of all the people who ever lived in the world, the Last Judgment, the Archangel Gabriel will blow his horn to call everyone together. All the angels will then stand with God to welcome the elect to heaven.

Since angels have through the centuries brought messages from God in heaven to men and women on earth, angels are sometimes pictured as having wings. Angels sometimes give a person a message while he or she is sleeping. Joseph was told in his sleep to take Mary as his wife. Later an angel directed Joseph to take his family to Egypt and after the danger had passed to return to Israel. At times an angel has taken the form of a man and has talked to a person face-to-face. For example, Zechariah was told by an angel that he would soon have a son. Mary Magdalene met two angels at the tomb of Jesus on the first Easter morning. They told her that Jesus had risen.

Artists have pictured the Archangel Michael in various ways. To some he has wings, to others he does not. He might be wearing a crown as the prince of the angels. He is pictured holding tightly to chains that are wrapped around Satan. He might be standing on top of a dragon, a symbol of Satan, and raising his sword in victory. He is often pictured as a young man, very strong, wearing battle armor, bare-legged, and with sandals on his feet.

The Archangel Michael, the protector of the Jews in ancient Israel and the protector of Christians today, is the patron of soldiers, particularly paratroopers. In Italy he is the patron of the police. In Normandy, France, along the Atlantic Coast, stands the enormous shrine of Mont St. Michel. This shrine honors Michael as the patron of sailors, who pray to him for safety against the "perils of the sea." In southeastern Italy years ago people prayed to Michael for protection from pirates who ravaged the Mediterranean. The Egyptian Christians asked Michael's help in causing the Nile River to flood and bring life-giving water to their crops. St. Michael is also the patron of grocers, who use scales to weigh the fruits and vegetables and other goods they sell. Michael is even the patron of X-ray technicians, and, along with St. Boniface, he is the patron of Germany.

St. Michael's feast day on September 29, which he shares with Sts. Gabriel and Raphael, is sometimes called Michaelmas Day. The English often prepare a special dinner of goose on that day. In parts of that country, the people have a procession at church and bake a cake called St. Michael's bannock.

Of the archangels who bring messages from God to us, Gabriel seems to be the best known. Gabriel, the prophet Daniel of the Old Testament tells us, came to him as a man "in rapid flight" (Daniel 9:21) and explained to him the meaning of his visions. To Zechariah, Gabriel brought the news that at last he and Elizabeth would have a baby. And to the Blessed Mother, Gabriel brought the message that she would be the Mother of God. For that reason Gabriel is sometimes called the Angel of the Annunciation.

Gabriel's name in Hebrew means "hero

of God." St. Gabriel is the patron of all people who bring messages—postal, telephone, and telegraph workers, and radio and television announcers and employees. He is pictured as a young man with long hair, sometimes with a small jewelled crown on his head, richly robed, and carrying a scepter or staff, or, if not that, a lily.

Raphael, the third of this famous trio of archangels, is mentioned only in the book of the Old Testament named Tobit. There God sends him to cure the blindness of an old man named Tobit. In disguise as a young man, Raphael travels for several days with Tobit's son, who is named Tobiah, and helps him collect a large sum of money owed to Tobit.

Raphael also guides Tobiah to Sarah, a woman Tobiah marries. The money, Tobiah's inheritance from his parents, is a fitting wedding gift. And poor Sarah is happy at last. Her seven previous husbands had all been murdered by a "wicked demon named Asmodeus" on the night of their wedding. Raphael returns with Tobiah to his father, who is pleased with his son's good fortune. Before he leaves for heaven, Raphael tells Tobit that he is "one of the seven angels who enter and serve before the Glory of the Lord"

(Tobit 12:15). Shortly after Raphael gives that message, Tobit, who was blind for four years, regains his sight. He lives many more years to age 112.

An ancient tradition tells us how an angel would come down at certain times to the pool of Bethesda in Jerusalem and stir up the water. The first to go into the pool after the water was stirred up was cured of whatever sickness that person had. Tradition identifies this angel as Raphael. At that pool Jesus cured a paralyzed man, who had been lying there for thirty-eight years, unable to make his way quickly to the pool after the water was stirred up.

St. Raphael, the archangel who traveled with Tobiah, is the patron of travelers, the blind, nurses, physicians, and of happy meetings. People often pray to St. Raphael for a cure of a sickness. Many a hospital, health center, or nursing home is dedicated to this saint.

The Archangels Michael, Gabriel, and Raphael, and legions of other angels—the exact number no one knows—continue to sing praise to God in heaven. We join this marvelous music as we sing or say at Mass: "Holy, Holy, Holy, Lord God of power and might."

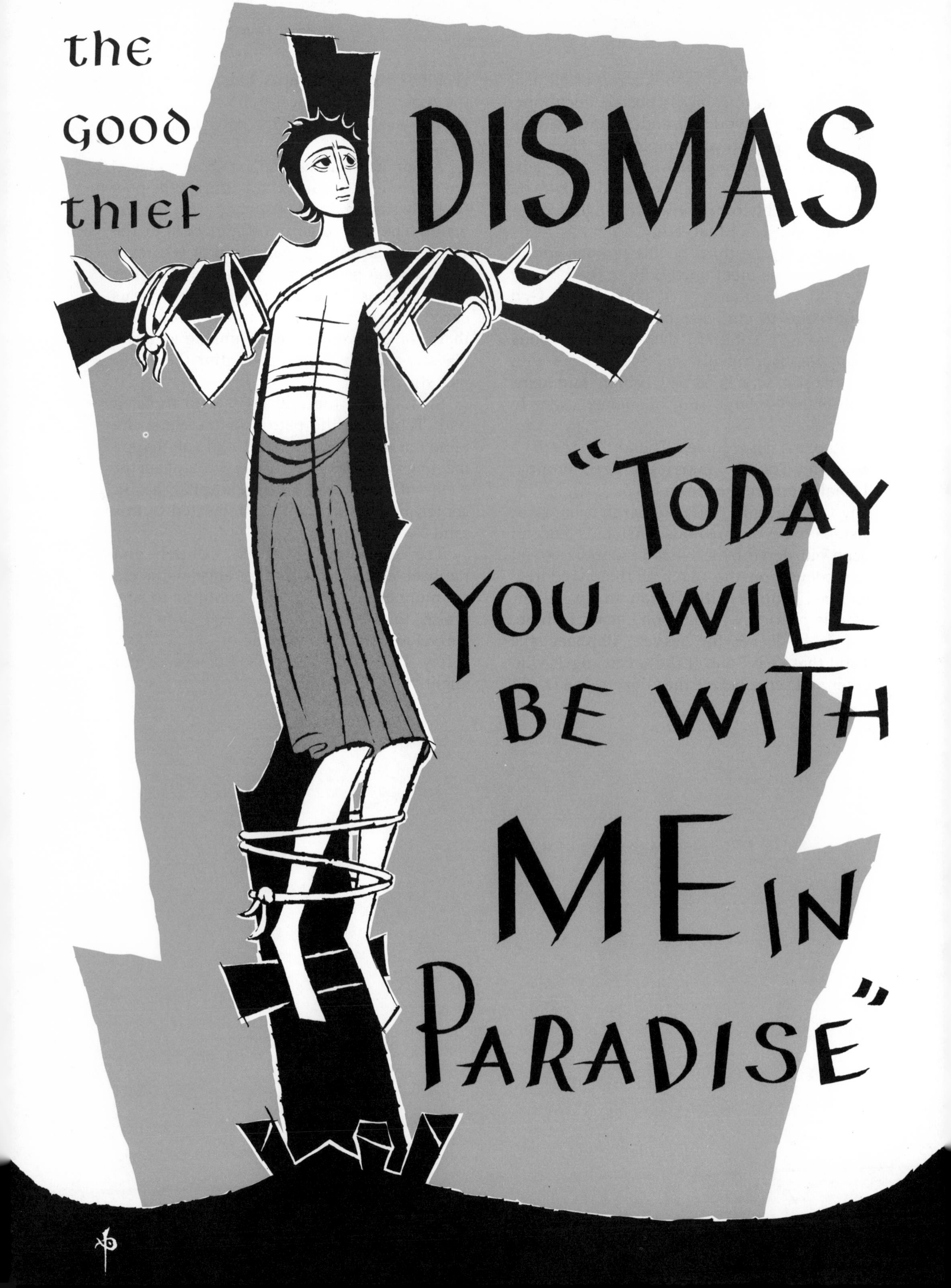
the good thief
DISMAS
"TODAY YOU WILL BE WITH ME IN PARADISE"

St. Dismas

On Friday in Holy Week, the week before Easter Sunday, the Christian world remembers in special church services and prayers the death of the Savior, Jesus Christ. On that Good Friday, Jesus by his death on the cross fulfilled the promise of salvation which God had made with his people. On that day Jesus opened the gateway to heaven to all who follow his teachings. It is a day of repentance as well as a day of celebration. The Son of God gave his life so that all men, women, and children everywhere in the world, now and for all time, may gain eternal life in heaven.

On either side of Jesus, as he hung dying on the cross on Mount Calvary, was another man condemned to death. These men were thieves and were sentenced to die because of their crimes. One of them was repentant of his sins and asked Jesus to forgive him so that he could enter heaven after he died. St. Luke's Gospel tells us about this man, who is commonly referred to as the Good Thief: "One of the criminals hanging there in crucifixion blasphemed him [Jesus]: 'Aren't you the Messiah? Then save yourself and us.' But the other one rebuked him: 'Have you no fear of God, seeing you are under the same sentence? We deserve it, after all. We are only paying the price for what we've done, but this man has done nothing wrong.' He then said, 'Jesus, remember me when you enter upon your reign.' And Jesus replied, 'I assure you: this day you will be with me in paradise'" (Luke 23:39-42).

Over the centuries the Good Thief came to be called Dismas. Some writers have called him Zoathan. Today Dismas is a patron of the dying, especially those condemned to death for crimes. The Good Thief is the model for all Christians of perfect contrition, of deep sorrow for having offended God. As he neared the end of his life, Dismas felt very sorry for the faults of his wayward years and asked Jesus for forgiveness. Jesus, the Son of God, willingly granted that forgiveness and assured the Good Thief that he would join him in God's heavenly kingdom. In this sense Dismas was the Good Thief. He had the goodness in his soul to repent of his sins and to ask for forgiveness.

Outside of St. Luke's Gospel account given above, we do not know

---

St. Dismas

First century, d. about A.D. 30
The Good Thief

Feast Day — formerly March 25

Meaning of name — dying, from the Greek *dysmē*

Latin
Dismas

English
Dismas
Dysmas
Desmas

---

any certain facts about Dismas. Legends about the earlier and criminal life of Dismas, however, do exist. One legend describes how two robbers named Titus and Dumachus stopped Mary and Joseph and the infant Jesus as they were making their way to Egypt. Shortly after the first Christmas the Holy Family fled Bethlehem, after the warning of an angel, to escape the hatred of King Herod. When Dumachus realized who it was that they were about to rob, he offered Titus forty silver coins if he would permit Joseph, Mary, and Jesus to continue on their journey unharmed. Reluctantly, Titus accepted the money and the Holy Family was spared. Thirty-three years later these two thieves were hung on either side of Jesus. Dumachus or Dismas was the Good Thief. Titus or Gestas was the other, the one who remained unrepentant.

Dismas lived an unruly life of crime and violence, but he died a holy death. He died next to Jesus, next to the Savior himself. He was the Good Thief who gained his salvation, like the rest of us, on Good Friday.

St. Dismas is also the patron of prisoners and funeral directors.

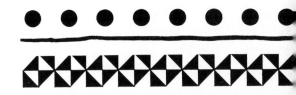

3. Apostles and Evangelists

St. Matthew

Almost two thousand years ago at Capernaum, a town in Galilee in the northern province of the Holy Land, a tax collector named Matthew worked in a customs house. There the local people came to pay their taxes to the Roman government, which then ruled Israel. Matthew's office looked out on the busy highway to Damascus, the capital of Syria. Merchants coming along that road had to stop at Matthew's desk to pay the customs or taxes they owed on the goods they were bringing into Capernaum. Matthew also calculated the tolls that travelers who used that highway owed the government. Most of the taxpayers did not like Matthew, simply because he was a tax collector and who likes to pay taxes? Besides, too often these officials were unfair, and to gain some extra cash for themselves they would charge too much for their services.

One day Jesus walked through Capernaum and noticed Matthew sitting at his desk in the customs house. Jesus said to him, "Follow me." Matthew immediately put away his account books and tax tables and joined Jesus as one of the twelve apostles. The apostles were Jesus' closest friends and became the first leaders of the Church after Jesus returned to heaven. Matthew was also known as Levi, the son of Alpheus. Beyond these facts, little for certain is known about Matthew.

For three years the apostles and other followers of Jesus witnessed the Lord's ministry as he preached the kingdom of his Father in heaven and worked miracles among the people of Israel. Then, after the apostles on the first Pentecost Day were blessed by the Holy Spirit and filled with energy to preach the Good News, they left their hiding

---

St. Matthew

First century

Apostle, Evangelist

Feast Day — September 21

Meaning of name — gift of God, from the Hebrew *mattithyāh*

Latin
Matthaeus

French
Mathieu

Spanish
Mateo

Italian
Matteo

German
Matthäus

Dutch
Mattheus

Norwegian
Matteus

English
Matthew
Mat
Matty
May f.

place in Jerusalem to proclaim this message about Jesus throughout Israel and even in distant lands. In time this proclamation of how Jesus, the Son of God, redeemed the world for all peoples, as well as many sayings of Jesus and the account of his life on earth, were recorded by writers directed by God. This written record is found in the New Testament, the second of the two main parts of the Bible. The inspired word of God, the Bible is the most important book in the world.

Four books called Gospels form the most familiar part of the New Testament. "Gospel" is an ancient English word meaning "god spell," which comes from the Greek word *euangelion.* Thus the writers of the Gospels are called evangelists.

The First Gospel was written by the evangelist whom we call Matthew. We do not know, however, who this Matthew was. It seems clear today that he was not the apostle by that name, nor was he an eyewitness to the events that are described in this Gospel. It was probably written during the 80s, about fifty years after Jesus died. While we do not know who the author of the First Gospel was, we do know from what he wrote that he was a Greek-speaking Christian or possibly a Greek-speaking Jewish-Christian who knew much about Jewish law and traditions. It seems that he lived in Syria, perhaps in Antioch. Matthew's Gospel is the first of the four Gospels because early scholars thought that it was the first written.

Each day at Mass the priest or deacon reads aloud for a few minutes from one of the Gospels. The homily that follows often comments on a particular teaching or event taken from the Gospel just read. If the Good News that day is from Matthew, the homilist might very well preach about the central message of the First Gospel. Matthew tells us most plainly that Jesus is the promised Savior, the Messiah through whom God fulfilled the promise he made to Abraham, Moses, Isaiah, and all of his Chosen People recorded in the Old Testament. Just like the Jewish people who followed God's law as expressed in the Old Testament, those who follow Jesus and the message of the New Testament are God's people.

The Gospel is directed largely at the Jewish-Christian community in which the evangelist lived, but also Matthew was most concerned that the non-Jewish people, the Gentiles, hear this Good News. It is only in Matthew's Gospel that the word *Church* appears—the community of Christians who help one another live according to Jesus' teachings.

The four Gospels, and particularly the first three, describe many of the same stories, teachings, and sayings of Jesus. Each of them, however, contains information that the others do not have. Matthew's, for example, is the only Gospel to record the parables of the weeds (13:24-30), the hidden treasure, the pearl, and the net (13:44-50), all of which describe the kingdom of heaven. Writes Matthew: "The kingdom of heaven is like a merchant's search for fine pearls. When he found one really valuable pearl, he went back and put up for sale all that he had and bought it" (13:45-46).

Matthew is the most quoted of the Gospels, not because it is first in the series, but because it records many sayings of Jesus. For example, Jesus urges: "Do not lay up for yourselves an earthly treasure. Moths and rust corrode; thieves break in and steal. Make it your practice instead to store up heavenly treasure, which neither moths nor rust corrode nor thieves break in and steal" (6:19-20).

A chapter earlier Jesus gives us the difficult message to love our enemies: "You have heard the commandment, 'You shall love your countryman but hate your enemy.' My command to you is: love your enemies, pray for your persecutors. This will prove that you are sons of your heavenly Father . . ." (5:43-45).

The final chapter of Matthew reports how after his resurrection Jesus told the apostles to preach the Good News throughout the world: "Go, therefore, and make disciples of all the nations. Baptize them in the name 'of the Father, and of the Son, and of the Holy Spirit.' Teach them to carry out everything I have commanded you. And know that I am with you always, until the end of the world!" (28:19-20). It is thought that the Apostle Matthew, in obeying that directive, spent many years preaching in Judea, the southern province of the Holy Land. Some writers say that he also preached in Prussia (northern Germany) or even in Macedonia (northern Greece).

Some scholars say that Matthew was martyred—perhaps burned, stoned, or even speared to death. Others say that he died a natural death. No one is certain where he was buried.

St. Matthew the Apostle is usually portrayed as an elderly man with a beard and holding a book of the Gospels in his hand.

Some artists have pictured Matthew with a purse or a money box, in reference to his work as a tax collector. Again, he is sometimes pictured with a sword, a spear, or an axe, references to his possible martyrdom. Since traditionally St. Matthew the Apostle was thought to be the same person as the author of the Gospel that bears his name, he is often pictured as a winged man. This symbol refers to the beginning of this Gospel, which lists the ancestors of Jesus. The wings symbolize Jesus' divinity as the Son of God; the image of a man symbolizes Jesus' human ancestry as the son of David, the Hebrew king.

St. Matthew is the patron of tax collectors, bankers, accountants, and bookkeepers.

St. Mark

In Venice, Italy, a city of 378 bridges connecting 117 small islands, a city where children ride boats rather than buses to school, is the famous St. Mark's Piazza. On one side of this huge square is a many-towered cathedral that is more than a thousand years old. Deep below the cathedral lies buried the body of St. Mark, the patron of the city. Next to and towering above the cathedral is a granite pillar. On its top is the statue of a winged lion. This lion is a symbol of St. Mark the Evangelist, whose Gospel begins with the story of St. John the Baptist crying in the wilderness (like a lion).

Two theories prevail regarding who wrote the Second Gospel. One holds that the author was the disciple John Mark, whom St. Peter called "my son Mark." He is often mentioned in the Book of Acts of the New Testament as the person who accompanied St. Paul and St. Barnabas (Mark's cousin) on missionary journeys. Other scholars contend that since Mark was such a common name in the first century the author was definitely a Christian by that name but perhaps not the disciple John Mark.

St. Mark

First century

Evangelist

Feast Day — April 25

Meaning of name — warlike, from the Latin *Mars, Martis*

Latin, Danish Dutch		*Italian*
Marcus		Marco
		Marcello
Greek		*English*
Markos		Mark
French		Marc
Marc		Marcus
Marcel		Marcius
Marcelle f.		Marcy
		Marcie
Spanish		Marcia
Marcos		Marcella f.
		Marsha
German		March
Markus		

The evangelist's major source for the Gospel was the large body of information about Jesus available in story form in the Christian communities in which he lived, perhaps in Rome or maybe in Syria or some other country in the Near East. It was written between A.D. 65 and 75. The first written Gospel, it was the major source of information for the Gospels of Matthew and Luke. It is the shortest Gospel, just 673 lines or verses.

The opening lines of the Gospel according to St. Mark announce that "this is the Good News about Jesus Christ, the Son of God" (1:1). Then, for sixteen short chapters, Mark tells us about Jesus' work in Israel, especially about the miracles he performed and about his last week in Jerusalem when he suffered and died on the cross. Mark

SAINT

MARK

PREACHER

AND

EVANGELIST

wrote in Greek, a language widely spoken in the Roman Empire during the first century. It is a simply written Gospel, using commonly understood words and a rather rugged sentence structure.

The Second Gospel drives home the message that it is no easy assignment to be a Christian. "If anyone wants to come with me, he must forget himself, carry his cross, and follow me," Jesus tells us (8:34). Even the apostles did not understand at first that Jesus had to suffer and die in order to bring salvation to the world. Mark wants his readers to be more willing than were the apostles to trust Jesus. We should be like the Roman army officer at the crucifixion, a stranger to Jesus until that meeting, who declared, "This man was really the Son of God" (15:39).

The author of Mark did a particularly good job of detailing the human side of Jesus. He tells us that Jesus did get angry when provoked. When the Jewish leaders did not want him to cure a man with a paralyzed hand because it was the sabbath, Jesus answered them, "Is it permitted to do a good deed on the sabbath—or an evil one? To preserve life—or to destroy it?" (3:4). Jesus became angry with the apostles for keeping little children from him. He told the apostles, "Let the children come to me and do not hinder them. It is to just such as these that the kingdom of God belongs" (10:14). Jesus saw the need at times to give simple, commonsense advice. When he raised the daughter of Jairus to life, Jesus told the little girl's parents to give her something to eat (5:43).

Mark's Gospel ends rather abruptly with the message from the angel guarding the empty tomb of Jesus to the holy women on Easter morning: "You need not be amazed! You are looking for Jesus of Nazareth, the one who was crucified. He has been raised up; he is not here. . . . Go now and tell his disciples and Peter: 'He is going ahead of you to Galilee, where you will see him just as he told you'" (16:6-7). The evangelist wants the readers of the Second Gospel, like the women at the empty tomb, to find Jesus in their own lives.

Like the Venetians, the people of Alexandria, Egypt, have a close association with St. Mark. It is believed that Mark preached the Gospel in that city and became their first bishop. He may also have preached the Good News in Libya and other North African lands, as well as in Aquileia, an ancient city on the Adriatic Sea.

It is said that Mark was martyred on the streets of Alexandria about the year 74. An angry mob bound him with a rope and dragged him over stones until he died. Some accounts say that his body was then burned. Others report that Mark was burned alive. Still other scholars are not certain that Mark was martyred.

Mark was buried in Alexandria in a marble tomb. There his body remained for almost eight hundred years. But in the year 815, merchants from Venice stole the saint's body from its tomb and brought it to their city. The doge, the ruler of Venice, ordered that a cathedral be built in the main square and that the saint's bones be secretly buried under one of the great pillars of that huge church. No one would ever steal them again.

St. Mark's feast day is April 25, a day of festive celebration in Venice. That city, which is situated on the northern Adriatic coast, is buffeted by frequent storms, and its citizens often call upon their patron for safety. Christians elsewhere, too, often ask St. Mark to intercede with God during lightning and hail storms. St. Mark is also the patron of notaries, those who keep official records. He is also the patron of glassworkers, a major industry in Venice, and lawyers.

St. Luke

"I thought it would be good to write an orderly account for you. I do this so that you will know the full truth about everything which you have been taught" (Luke 1:3-4). With these words St. Luke dedicates his Gospel to a man named Theophilus. Luke wanted him, and all his readers, to understand and live the Good News that the promised Savior brought to Israel and to the world.

Luke was a Gentile, that is, a person who is not Jewish. He grew up, it is thought, in Antioch, Syria, a country neighboring Israel on the north. Eventually Luke heard about the teachings of Jesus from the early Christians and joined the Church. Tradition tells us that he may have been a companion of St. Paul on several missionary journeys. St. Paul calls him "our dear physician" (Colossians 4:14), a reference to his profession.

Luke was not an eyewitness to the events of Jesus' life. The stories concerning the work of the Savior and the first years of the Church that were told by Christians for about a half century, as well as written sources such as St. Mark's Gospel, provided this evangelist the information for his pen. The Third Gospel is an account of the Christian story from the announcement that John the Baptist would be born to the ascension of Jesus to heaven. The Gospel was written some time during the 80s. Luke was particularly concerned that his fellow Gentiles hear the Good News. He called Jesus the "light to the Gentiles" (2:32).

Luke also wrote the Acts of the Apostles, which could be called volume 2 of the Third Gospel. There he tells us much about the growth and spread of the Christian faith after the ascension of Jesus to about the year 63. During this period Christianity, despite years of vicious persecution, spread throughout Israel and to Syria, Greece, Italy, and to other countries of the Roman Empire. Many of the hard times that St. Paul and his followers faced, such as shipwreck and imprisonment, are described in Acts. In the Bible, Acts is positioned

---

St. Luke

First century

Evangelist

Feast Day — October 18

Meaning of name — light, from the Greek *loukas*

Latin, Spanish
Lucas

French
Luc

Italian
Luca

German, Norwegian
Lukas

English
Luke
Luck
Lucky

65

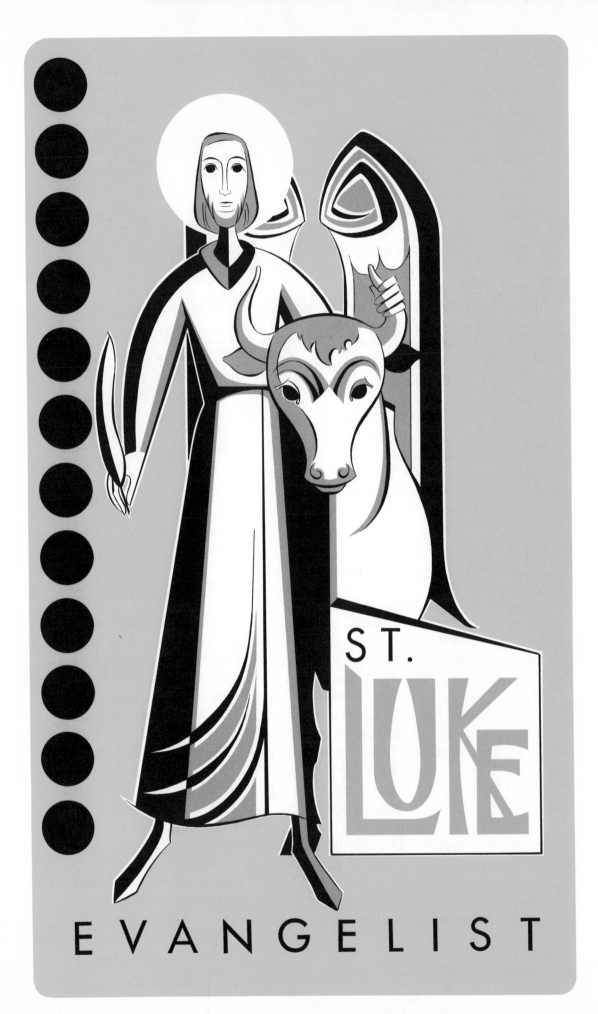

ST. LUKE

EVANGELIST

directly after the four Gospels. Luke wrote more pages of the New Testament than did any other writer.

Luke's Gospel, as well as Matthew's, records Jesus' birth at Bethlehem. The account read at Midnight Mass on Christmas Eve is perhaps the most familiar passage from Luke. It begins: "In those days Caesar Augustus published a decree ordering a census of the whole world. This first census took place while Quirinius was governor of Syria. Everyone went to register, each to his own town" (2:1-3). Then follows the carefully wrought portrait of the birth of Jesus in the stable—"because there was no room for them in the place where travelers lodged" (2:7).

Luke's Gospel includes the account of six miracles and eighteen parables that the other evangelists do not mention. Among the parables are the famous stories of the Prodigal Son and the Good Samaritan. The account of Zacchaeus, the tax collector who climbed a sycamore tree in order to see Jesus as he passed through Jericho, is also peculiar to this Gospel. Jesus noticed this short man peering at him and told him, "'Zacchaeus, hurry down. I mean to stay at your house today.' He quickly descended, and welcomed him with delight. When this was observed, everyone began to murmur, 'He has gone to a sinner's house as a guest'" (19:5-6). Luke's Gospel stresses that Jesus made a special effort to help sinners.

In fact, this Gospel is sometimes called the Gospel of Great Pardons because it reports many occasions when Jesus forgave people their sins. For example, when Jesus cured a paralytic, he did not just tell the man, "Get up and walk." He also said, "Your sins are forgiven you" (5:23). Zacchaeus, too, like Matthew, was forgiven for having cheated people on their taxes. In the Lord's Prayer, reported in chapter 11, we ask God to "forgive us our sins, for we too forgive all who do us wrong." Jesus reminds us that we must forgive our brother and sister if we wish to be forgiven (17:3-4).

The gentleness of Jesus is another familiar theme of the Third Gospel. In the parable of the unfruitful fig tree, for example, a gardener convinces the owner of an orchard not to cut down the tree. "Sir, leave it another year, while I hoe around it and manure it; then perhaps it will bear fruit. If not, it shall be cut down" (13:8-9). Similarly, the account of Jesus raising the widow of Nain's son to life reflects the Lord's gentleness. When Jesus saw the weeping widow and mother, he told her not to cry. Then he touched the coffin and told the young man to get up. "The dead man sat up and began to speak. Then Jesus gave him back to his mother" (7:15).

Luke is also known as the Evangelist of Prayer. He reports how often Jesus prayed to his Father in heaven—at his baptism, before he chose the apostles, when he was transfigured on Mount Tabor, when he prayed on the Mount of Olives the night before he died, etc. When the apostles asked how they might pray, Jesus taught them the Lord's Prayer.

Frequently, an ox is a symbol of Luke because his Gospel begins and ends with references to the Temple in Jerusalem. There the Jews sacrificed oxen to God. The last passage of this Gospel tells us that after Jesus' ascension to heaven, the disciples "fell down to do him reverence, then returned to Jerusalem filled with joy. There they were to be found in the temple constantly, speaking the praises of God" (24:52-53). The goal of every Christian is to join Jesus and his Father in the heavenly Jerusalem.

Artists have pictured Luke painting a portrait of the Blessed Mother. While it is doubtful that Luke met Mary, it is certain that his written portraits tell us much about her. Some famous prayers associated with Mary, such as the *Magnificat* and the first part of the Hail Mary, are recorded in his Gospel.

Luke never married nor did he become a priest. He is one of the first great laymen of the Church. He died at age eighty-four in Thebes, Greece. About the year 357 his body was brought to Constantinople, now Istanbul, Turkey. Later his body was reburied in the Church of St. Justina in Padua, Italy.

Like St. Mark, St. Luke is the patron of glassworkers and notaries. He is also the patron of physicians, painters, and butchers.

St. John the Apostle

When St. John the Apostle was a very old man and could not walk, his friends would carry him to the church in Ephesus. In this ancient city in what is present-day Turkey, John spent many years preaching the Good News. There in the church John would talk to the Ephesians about his love of God and the Christian faith.

John wanted both children and adults to realize that it was love that brought Jesus to us as the Savior. It is through love of God and neighbor that a person shares the life of Jesus. John knew that seeing the Lord in every person one meets each day is the best possible approach to God.

St. John the Apostle

First century, d. A.D. 101

Apostle, Evangelist

Feast Day — December 27

For other name forms of John, *see* story about St. John Neumann on p. 20.

It was from John the Baptist that John the Apostle learned about Jesus. One day the Apostle heard the Baptizer preach about the Savior who would soon draw crowds whenever he spoke. It was not long afterward that Jesus stopped along the Sea of Galilee to visit John and his older brother James. They, along with their father and a hired man, were mending the fish nets used in the family business. Jesus asked the two Zebedee brothers to follow him and to learn how to "catch men" (Matthew 4:19). Jesus was asking them to help him preach the Good News about the kingdom of heaven. The brothers immediately dropped their nets and joined Jesus. Since they had fiery tempers, Jesus called the Zebedee brothers "sons of thunder" (Mark 3:17). But that was only one side of John's personality. He also was a warmhearted, gentle person.

John was with Jesus at several important events that many or even all of the other apostles did not witness. With his brother James and Peter, John saw Jesus raise the daughter of Jairus to life. These three apostles also were with Jesus on Mount Tabor when God the Father spoke to Jesus from heaven. The same three apostles stayed with Jesus the evening before he died. There in the Garden of Gethsemane Jesus prayed, but the apostles fell asleep.

Jesus sent John and Peter to order the food and to prepare the dining room for the Last Supper. On that first Holy Thursday evening, Jesus changed bread and wine into his body and blood. At that meal he said good-bye to his apostles because he knew that the next day he would die. Also to one of the apostles, who is alleged to be John, Jesus revealed that Judas Iscariot would betray him. When the soldiers brought Jesus to the palace of Annas, the father-in-law of the high

SAINT

JOHN

APOSTLE

priest Caiaphas, an unnamed apostle followed the Lord into the courtyard. That apostle may have been John. Peter went along to the palace too, but at first he waited at the gate.

The next day, the first Good Friday, John was the only apostle to stay at the foot of the cross until Jesus died. Moments before he died Jesus asked John to take care of Mary his Mother. And on Easter Sunday "the other disciple (the one Jesus loved)," mentioned in the Fourth Gospel (20:2), who arrives at Jesus' empty tomb, traditionally has been identified as John.

John and Peter preached the gospel in Samaria, the central province of the Holy Land. Later John preached in Ephesus and other communities in Asia Minor. For a while the Roman government banished John to the island of Patmos in the Aegean Sea. A story is told that before John was exiled, the Emperor Domitian had John thrown into a cauldron of boiling oil in Rome before the Latin Gate, but John miraculously was not harmed.

St. Epiphanius has told us that after his exile on Patmos John returned to Ephesus, where he lived to age ninety-four. He died in the year 101 during the reign of the Emperor Trajan. It is believed that John was buried in Ephesus.

For centuries the Fourth Gospel, the Gospel according to John, was regarded as the work of John the Apostle, the son of Zebedee. Recent work of scholars makes it clear, however, that John did not directly write this Gospel. Rather, it was written somewhere between A.D. 80 and 100, it is thought, by disciples of John who were familiar with the teachings of this eyewitness to Jesus' public life of preaching and healing among the people of Israel.

The message of the Fourth Gospel is clearly put in chapter 20: "Jesus performed many other signs as well—signs not recorded here—in the presence of his disciples. But these have been recorded to help you believe that Jesus is the Messiah, the Son of God, so that through this faith you may have life in his name" (30-31). That faith will be strengthened by the Holy Spirit, a mysterious force like the wind—felt but not completely understood—whom God sent so that we may always feel the presence of Jesus. The Spirit is the bond of love which unites Christians to one another and to Jesus.

The Gospel's first chapter describes how Jesus, whom John calls the Word, "became a human being and, full of grace and truth, lived among us. We saw his glory, the glory which he received as the Father's only Son" (1:14). Twenty chapters later the Gospel concludes with the startling message: "Now, there are many other things that Jesus did. If they were all written down one by one, I suppose that the whole world could not hold the books that would be written" (21:25).

Artists often picture St. John the Apostle with a chalice and a snake. A legend tells how once John was about to drink from a chalice, but all of a sudden a snake uncurled out of it. The chalice had held poison. Another symbol of St. John is an eagle because the language and thought of the beginning of the Gospel that bears his name soars to the heights, like an eagle, as it speaks about Jesus.

The English and the Greeks call this saint John "the Divine" because he was so filled with the teachings about God that Jesus revealed to him. He is the patron of theologians, Asia Minor, and good friendships. His help is sought for protection against burns and poisons. Sometimes, too, he is known as John of Patmos.

St. Peter

The heart of Vatican City, the tiny nation within Rome, Italy, that is the home for the Holy Father, the Pope, is St. Peter's Basilica. About sixty feet to one side of the main altar in this famous church is a bronze statue of St. Peter. This saint, sometimes called the Prince of the Apostles, was the first bishop of Rome and the first head of the Church. On this statue, which is attributed to the sculptor Arnolfo di Cambrio, the right foot of the saint extends a few inches out from its pedestal. Daily hundreds of visitors to the basilica reverently walk up to the statue and kiss St. Peter's foot. So many people have paid that mark of respect to this great saint that the foot of St. Peter has been partially kissed away.

That bronze sculpture and other likenesses of Peter show this saint holding two or three keys. The keys refer to an important conversation that Jesus had

St. Peter

First century, d. A.D. 64 or 65

Apostle, first bishop of Rome

Feast Day — June 29

Meaning of name — rock, from the Greek *petros*

Latin	*Russian*
Petrus	**Piotr**
	Petr
French	
Pierre	*Norwegian*
Perry	**Peter**
Pierette f.	
	English
Spanish, Portuguese	**Peter**
Pedro	**Pete**
	Peterkin
Italian	**Pierce**
Pietro	**Pierson**
German	
Petrus	
Peter	

with Peter and the other eleven apostles. One day Jesus asked them, "Who do you say I am?" Peter answered, "You are the Messiah, the Son of the living God." Then Jesus told Peter, "You are a rock, and on this rock foundation I will build my church . . . . I will give you the keys of the Kingdom of heaven. . . ." (Matthew 16:15-16, 18-19).

That is how Jesus told Peter that he was to lead the apostles and the entire world in understanding and following his teachings. Soon after Jesus ascended to heaven, the Holy Spirit came to the apostles on the first Pentecost Day and confirmed them. From then on the apostles had the strength to preach the gospel far and wide. For many years Peter led the apostles in that work, which continues to this very day. In 1978 Pope John Paul II became the 264th successor to St. Peter as the bishop of Rome and the leader of the Church on this earth. Since the Pope continues St. Peter's work, some writers say that the Holy Father "sits in St. Peter's chair."

Peter as a youngster lived in Bethsaida, a town in the province of

SAINTS
PETER AND
PAUL
APOSTLES

Galilee in the Holy Land. But he did not answer to the name of Peter. His parents called him Simon. He grew up to be a commercial fisherman on the Sea of Galilee. With his brother Andrew and their partners, the Zebedee brothers James and John, they made a good living catching and selling fish.

One day Andrew rushed home very excited after having heard John the Baptist preach about the coming of the Savior. That particular day John recognized Jesus in the crowd and pointed him out to the people. As soon as possible, Andrew took his brother to meet Jesus. At that meeting Jesus told Peter, "Your name is Simon son of John, but you will be called Cephas" (John 1:42). That name is the same as "Peter," which means "rock." Not until some months later did Peter realize the significance of his new name. He was to be the leader, the rock, that Jesus would put in charge of his Church when he returned to God the Father in heaven.

Peter and Andrew kept fishing each day, but they also listened to Jesus preach whenever they could. Then one day Jesus came to where they were casting a net into the water. He told them, "Come with me, and I will teach you to catch men" (Matthew 4:19). Immediately they dropped their work and went with Jesus. From then on Peter and Andrew served the Lord as apostles. They carefully listened to him, learning the truths of his gospel, and they witnessed miracle upon miracle that Jesus performed. They became "fishers of men" and devoted their lives to teaching others about Jesus. In Jerusalem on that first Pentecost Day alone, Peter preached such a powerful sermon that almost three thousand people joined the Church.

Peter's name always comes first in the various lists of the apostles in the New Testament. That in itself indicates his importance. Also many incidents in the Gospels single out Peter. It was Peter who first told Jesus that he knew that Jesus was the Son of God. On Easter Sunday Peter was the first apostle to enter the empty tomb. It was from Peter's boat that Jesus preached to the huge crowd

gathered on the shore of the Sea of Galilee. One time Jesus went to Peter's house in Capernaum and cured Peter's mother-in-law of a fever. Another time, when Jesus and Peter were discussing the paying of the Temple tax, Jesus sent Peter to catch a fish. There in the mouth of that fish Peter found a coin of enough value to pay the tax for both himself and Jesus. One day after the first Pentecost, it was Peter who cured a lame beggar that he and the Apostle John met outside the Temple. Peter told the poor man, "I have neither silver nor gold, but what I have I give you! In the name of Jesus Christ the Nazorean, walk!" (Acts 3:6).

Like anyone, Peter had a few faults. Sometimes he acted before he thought. He was demanding. At least on one occasion he was untruthful, for which he was terribly sorry. Peter was with Jesus when the Savior was arrested in the Garden of Gethsemane the night before he died. Without thinking, Peter pulled out his sword and cut off the right ear of Malchus, a servant of the high priest. Fortunately for Malchus, Jesus touched the ear and it healed immediately.

Once Peter reminded Jesus that the apostles had given up their careers and their families to follow him. Peter was wondering what Jesus would give them in return. Later, when Peter understood the meaning of the kingdom of heaven, he felt differently. Peter was then certain that he never would deny that he knew Jesus, and he told Jesus so the night of the Last Supper. But Jesus answered Peter, "I tell you that before the rooster crows tonight, you will say three times that you do not know me" (Matthew 26:34). Sure enough. After Jesus was arrested, three people at different times asked Peter if he knew Jesus. He told them that he never heard of the man. At the moment of the third denial, Peter heard a rooster crow. The Gospel according to Matthew tells us that "he went out and wept bitterly" (26:75).

Peter was a born leader. The apostles and the other early Christians could depend on him to solve problems. Shortly after Jesus ascended into heaven, Peter called the apostles together to choose a successor to

Judas Iscariot, the apostle who had betrayed Jesus for thirty pieces of silver. Once, when all the apostles were arrested, Peter spoke to the officials in their defense. It was Peter who baptized the first non-Jews or Gentiles that joined the Church. In the year 50 Peter presided at the very important Council of the Apostles. Peter preached the gospel wherever he traveled, not only in the Holy Land but also in Greece, Syria, Italy, and Asia Minor. Sometimes Peter sent instructions to the new Christian communities by letter.

In the year 42 the cruel governor of Judea, Herod Agrippa I, wanted to kill Peter. The governor had ordered many Christians executed, including the Apostle James, who was Peter's lifelong friend and former fishing partner. The governor had Peter tossed into prison, where he was bound in chains. A guard sat on either side of the prisoner, and sentries kept watch at the door of his cell. But at this time God had plans other than martyrdom for Peter. He sent an angel to set him free.

Peter spent his last years, exactly how many we do not know, in Rome. He was the first bishop of that huge pagan city, the capital of the mighty Roman Empire. There amidst great danger he, St. Paul, and other early leaders of the Church preached the gospel and made many converts. For his decision to follow Jesus, rather than the Roman gods—Jupiter, Mercury, Venus, Apollo, and dozens of others—Peter paid with his life. During the reign of Emperor Nero, Peter was crucified, probably in the year 64 or 65. Some historians give the date as June 29, 64. At his request, Peter was crucified with his head downwards. Emperor Nero killed Christians as if they were mosquitoes, but still thousands of Romans joined the Church.

For a time the body of the Prince of the Apostles seems to have been buried in the catacombs near Rome. From as early as the second century, there is evidence that his body was reburied in Rome at a place called the Vatican. There in the fourth century, Constantine the Great, the Christian emperor, built the first St. Peter's Basilica. Twelve hundred years later the present magnificent basilica was constructed on the same spot. Deep below its main altar lies the grave of the Prince of the Apostles. The basilica is not only the tomb of St. Peter and of other popes. It is also the largest and the most important church in Christendom.

St. Peter is the patron of locksmiths and shoemakers.

St. Paul

It is a rarity that a man who persecuted Christians would suddenly become a great defender of the gospel message. During the year 34, in the first years of the Church, such an event happened to a man named Saul. While on his way (perhaps on horseback, as artists frequently suggest) to Damascus, Syria, to arrest Christians, Saul was suddenly thrown to the ground and blinded by a brilliant flash of light. A voice asked him, "Saul, Saul, why do you persecute me?" Saul answered, "Who are you, sir?" The voice said, "I am Jesus, the one you are persecuting" (Acts 9:4-5).

From that moment Saul was converted to Christianity. Jesus told him to continue to Damascus and find a man named Ananias who would baptize him. Saul did that and after a few days the blindness left him. With the return of his sight and the strength of his new faith, Saul, who was now called Paul, turned to a life of preaching and writing about the Good News. Paul preached especially to non-Jewish people, the Gentiles. He is known as the Apostle to the Gentiles.

St. Paul

First Century, d. A.D. 64 or 67

Apostle to the Gentiles

Feast Days — January 25
June 29

Meaning of name — little, from the Latin *paulus* or the Greek *paulos*

French
Paul
Paule
Pauline f.

Spanish
Pablo
Paulina f.

Italian
Paolo
Paolina f.

Portuguese
Paulo

German
Paul
Paulus

Paula
Paulina f.
Pauline

Russian
Pavel

Norwegian
Paulus

English
Paul
Paula
Pauline f.
Paulette

Paul was born to Jewish parents in Tarsus, a city in what is now Turkey. Since Tarsus was part of the Roman Empire, Paul was a Roman citizen. In fact, his name "Paul" is the Roman equivalent of the Jewish form of "Saul." Paul's parents sent him to school in Jerusalem, where he took classes from a famous teacher named Gamaliel. Paul studied hard and grew up to be a scholar of the Jewish religion. It upset him that many Jews chose to follow Jesus and become Christians. That's why Paul persecuted the Christians. He was among those in Jerusalem who stoned to death St. Stephen, who is the first martyr.

For about ten years following his conversion, Paul lived a quiet life of prayer and study. He met occasionally with the Apostles James and

75

Peter, who taught him much about Jesus and his Church. Peter recognized Paul's talents as an organizer and a preacher and convinced him to become a missionary.

For the next twenty years Paul crisscrossed the Mediterranean world, preaching in Palestine, Syria, Turkey, Greece, Italy, and elsewhere. He established communities of Christians in Antioch, Athens, Rome, Corinth, Ephesus, Thessalonika, and other cities, both big and small. In Antioch, for example, Paul, along with Barnabas, spent a whole year instructing the people about the teachings of Jesus. It was in Antioch that the citizens began to call the followers of Jesus "Christians"—the term had not been used before. The word *Christos* is the Greek translation of the Aramaic word *Mēsihā* (Messiah), the "anointed one."

When Paul could not personally pay a return visit to a city, at least for a long time, he often wrote letters or epistles to the Christians in those places. In his letters Paul advised the people how to solve their problems and encouraged them to lead Christian lives. His letters, which often were elaborate compositions, now form at least seven books of the New Testament. On almost every Sunday at Mass, a part of one of Paul's epistles is read. Paul's wisdom and advice may thus be appreciated today as it was in the first century by the Romans, the Corinthians, the Galatians, the Philippians, and other Christians.

Paul was not the easiest man to get along with. James once told him bluntly to be more tactful, more considerate of others. Mark and Barnabas once refused to join Paul on a journey because of an argument. But, like most people, Paul's good points outweighed his faults. His fellow Christians, such as Timothy, Titus, Silas, Luke, and the apostles and disciples who knew him, appreciated his good works.

Most of Paul's former Jewish friends could not accept Paul's conversion to Christianity. They regarded Paul as a traitor. Several times he narrowly escaped death; once he was stoned and left for dead. He was whipped; he was banished from several cities. Often Paul's missionary journeys were burdensome and dangerous experiences.

In the year 59, while Paul was preaching in Jerusalem, the Jews arrested him. Paul spent about four years in prison, first in Palestine, and then, as he was a Roman citizen, in Rome where he was brought for trial. While traveling there, Paul was shipwrecked near Malta, a good-sized island in the Mediterranean, during a hurricane.

Paul, other prisoners, and the Roman soldiers braved the storm and swam safely to shore. The local people treated them kindly and built a fire for them to warm up. While Paul was placing sticks on that fire, a snake jumped out of the flames and bit his hand. The Maltese people expected that Paul's hand would immediately swell up and that he would suddenly fall down and die. Paul, however, shook off the snake into the fire and was not harmed. Today St. Paul is remembered as the patron of Malta, as well as the patron against poisonous snakes.

Eventually, in Rome, Paul was released from prison, but in time he was arrested again, simply because he was a Christian. During the persecution of the Christians in the year 64 or 67 under Emperor Nero, Paul was beheaded for his faith.

Today pilgrims to Rome visit the Basilica of St. Paul Outside the Walls. This huge and magnificent church was built in the fourth century by the Emperor Constantine over the site of Paul's martyrdom and grave. The basilica is just a short walk from the walls of the old part of the city, thus its name. In the courtyard in front of the basilica is a famous statue of St. Paul.

The martyrs Peter and Paul share a feast day on June 29. A separate day, January 25, honors St. Paul's conversion to Christianity. Yet another feast day, November 18, celebrates the dedication of the Churches of St. Peter and St. Paul in Rome.

St. Paul is also the patron of ropemakers, tentmakers, and saddlemakers. As a young man, and off and on years later, Paul sewed tents for a living.

the CON-
VERSION
of ST.
PAUL

4. Martyrs

St. John the Baptist

John is the most popular boy's name in all Christendom. Dozens of saints are named John, and one of the most famous of them and the first so named is John the Baptist.

The Bible tells us much about John the Baptist, including many facts about his birth. His father, St. Zechariah, was a priest of the Temple in Jerusalem. His mother, St. Elizabeth, was a kinswoman of Mary, the Mother of Jesus.

Zechariah and Elizabeth wanted a baby very much, but years passed without a son or a daughter being born to them. One day

St. John the Baptist

First century

Precursor of Jesus, the Messiah

Feast Days — June 24
August 29

For other name forms of John, *see* story about St. John Neumann on p. 20.

when Zechariah was at his duties in the Temple offering incense to God, the Archangel Gabriel appeared to him and told Zechariah that he would soon have a son who should be named John. Zechariah could harldy believe the news, so he asked the angel for a sign that indeed this was true. Both as a sign and as a punishment for his disbelief, Gabriel then told Zechariah that he would be unable to speak until the baby was born.

Some months passed and a baby boy was born to Elizabeth. Eight days later his parents took their son to the Temple for the Jewish ceremony called circumcision. Elizabeth and other relatives and friends wanted to name the baby after his father, but Zechariah would not hear of it. He motioned for a tablet of paper and a pencil and wrote "His name is John" (Luke 1:63). Immediately thereafter Zechariah could again talk. His first words were a prayer of thanks to God for the gift of a child. That famous prayer, the *Benedictus,* is still prayed today.

The Bible tells of a famous meeting of the mothers of Jesus and John before either baby was born. At this meeting, now remembered as the Visitation (feast day on May 31), the two women shared each other's happiness that they would soon be mothers. Elizabeth greeted Mary, "Blest are you among women and blest is the fruit of your womb" (Luke 1:42). These words, which are part of the Hail Mary, have been said in prayer for centuries.

The lives of Jesus and John crossed most significantly when they were adults. It was John, in fact, who prepared the way for Jesus' public life of preaching his gospel to the Jews. John was the precursor (forerunner or announcer) of the Messiah. For years John had lived alone in the desert of Judea preparing for these duties. There he ate

saint

John the Baptist

grasshoppers and wild honey and wore clothes made out of camel's hair.

At age thirty John began preaching to the people who lived near the desert, urging them to repent of their sins. He told them that the Savior, the Messiah, would soon come to them. John was "a herald's voice in the desert, crying, 'Make ready the way of the Lord, clear him a straight path'" (Mark 1:3). John baptized the people with water as a sign that they would accept the kingdom of the Messiah. Crowds of people from all walks of life followed this powerful preacher. They listened to John and were baptized. The Apostles Andrew and John first heard about the Messiah from John the Baptist. Even the king, Herod Antipas, listened to John.

Some people thought that John himself was the Messiah, the Savior of the world. But John told them that he was not even worthy to untie the Messiah's shoelace. He said that the Savior was far greater and that he would baptize them with the Holy Spirit. John called Jesus the "Lamb of God." One day John noticed Jesus in the crowd near him at the edge of the River Jordan. That day Jesus insisted that John baptize him in the river. Many artists have painted that famous baptism.

King Herod admired the Baptizer and considered him a good man, but he also feared him because John told the truth about the king's sinful marriage. Herod had married his brother's wife while his brother was working in Rome. She was a beautiful but evil woman named Herodias. To please her the king eventually ordered his soldiers to arrest John and to haul him off to prison. Even behind bars John continued to preach and to urge everyone who could hear him to follow Jesus. From his cell he shouted out this message so loudly that Herod and Herodias could hear him even though their palace was some distance away.

One evening at a birthday party for Herod, his wife's attractive daughter Salome pleased the king with her dancing. Herod then promised Salome that he would give her anything she would ask for, even one-half of his kingdom. Salome could not begin to decide on this matter, so she asked her mother for help. Herodias by now was most anxious to get rid of John the Baptist because his goodness made her feel guilty. She told Salome to ask for the head of the Baptizer to be brought to her on a dish. Salome did just that.

King Herod was aghast at Salome's gruesome request, but nevertheless he ordered his soldiers to behead the Baptizer. The soldiers rushed off to the Fortress of Machaerus where John lingered. A short while later they returned to the party with John's head on a platter. Salome received the gift she had asked for. King Herod long regretted having ordered this murder. He himself died a painful death some years later after a lengthy illness.

The saint's followers buried John the Baptist's body in a tomb at Sebaste, about a day's journey from Jerusalem. Years later, during the reign of the Roman emperor Julian the Apostate, a pagan, the grave was destroyed.

The Church celebrates two feast days honoring St. John the Baptist. June 24 remembers his birth and August 29 his beheading. Only a few saints are honored by two or more feast days.

St. John the Baptist is the patron of bird dealers, tailors, and farriers, that is, blacksmiths who shoe horses. Many call upon his help for protection from hail storms, and farmers, ranchers, and shepherds ask St. John the Baptist to protect their lambs from danger.

St. Lucy

December 13, about midway through Advent, is St. Lucy Day. It is most appropriate that the feast day of this fourth-century martyr occurs during the season in which Christians prepare for Christmas. St. Lucy's name means "light." She reminds us that Jesus, the Savior, is the true light that enlightens every person born into the world.

St. Lucy Day celebrates light. In Scandinavia, where the summer brings the midnight sun and the winter long, long nights, families burn "Lucy candles" in their homes and "Lucy fires" outside. Formerly, when St. Lucy Day was celebrated on December 21, the shortest day of the year, people thanked the "light saint" whose day brought an end to the winter's darkest night. "Lucy-light, the shortest day and the longest night," children would sing.

In Sweden on St. Lucy Day, young girls put on long dresses and on their heads wear a wreath with five lighted candles called *levande lijus* or "living candles." For the Swedes that day marks the start of the Christmas season. Yellow buns called *leissi katten* or "St. Lucy's cats" are baked in the form of cats—with raisins as the eyes—and enjoyed as a special treat.

Little for sure is known about St. Lucy. We do know that she was the daughter of wealthy and noble parents in Syracuse, Sicily. As a young woman, perhaps yet a teenager, she was martyred on December 13, 304, during the persecution of the cruel Roman emperor Diocletian. We know too that from the time of Pope St. Gregory I in the sixth century St. Lucy's name has been among the martyrs mentioned in the first Eucharistic Prayer of the Mass. This tells us that St. Lucy has long been one of the most revered of the early martyrs.

While there are few facts about St. Lucy, many legends about her have been told for centuries. One of them, a story written both in prose and verse by the English writer St. Aldhem in the seventh century, describes her martyrdom.

St. Lucy

Fourth century

b. ?

d. **December 13, 304**

Feast Day — December 13

Meaning of name — light, from the Latin *lucia*

French	Norwegian
Lucie	Lucie
Lucille	*English*
Spanish	Lucy
Lucía	Lucia
Luz	Lucille
Italian	Lucinda
Lucia	Lucasta
German	Luzette
Lucia	Lulu
Luzia	Cindy

As a young girl Lucy promised God that she would not marry. Rather, she wanted to devote her life to God as a single person and to give the fortune she would inherit to the poor in Syracuse. Lucy, however, did not at first tell her mother about this promise. Not knowing of it, Eutychia arranged for Lucy to marry a young man, who happened to be a pagan.

One day her husband-to-be came to Eutychia's house to take her beautiful daughter as his bride. That day, however, Lucy had traveled to the nearby town of Catania to pray at the tomb of the martyr St. Agnes, praying particularly that her mother would be cured of a hemorrhage, a bleeding problem that afflicted her. God granted that cure.

Upon her return to Syracuse, Lucy found her mother cured and most happy. When she told Eutychia about her promise of virginity, her mother understood, but the waiting young man did not. He stormed out of the house and immediately informed the governor that Lucy was a Christian. Lucy was then called to a courtroom and commanded to worship the false gods of the Romans. When she refused, the judge ordered that from then on she must live in a house of prostitution.

But when the soldiers tried to drag Lucy from the courtroom, they could not make her move an inch. An invisible force bound her to the very spot where she stood during her trial. Even a team of oxen could not drag her away. The judge then ordered a bonfire to be built around her, but that too failed. Lucy remained alive, praising God, in spite of the flames. Finally, in desperation, a soldier pierced her throat with a dagger and Lucy died a martyr's death.

That legend suggests why some painters have pictured St. Lucy kneeling before a tomb or yoked to a pair of oxen. Other artists portray her in the company of St. Agnes, St. Agatha, and other virgin martyrs. Still others represent her with a dagger or a sword piercing her throat, from which come rays of light. Sometimes she is pictured holding a palm branch—a symbol of martyrdom—in one hand and a burning lamp in the other. Instead of a lamp she might be holding a book, a dish, or a shell, on which rest two eyes.

Two legends explain why Lucy holds her own eyes. One tells how the executioner blinded her. Another mentions that St. Lucy herself plucked out her eyes and presented them to her husband-to-be, who admired their immense beauty. In both legends God restored her sight, and her eyes were more beautiful than before. Understandably, then, St. Lucy is the patron of those who suffer from eye problems. People who injure their eyes or have a disease of the eye pray to God through St. Lucy to have light restored to their body.

St. Lucy is also the patron of at least five other causes and places: the city of Syracuse, schoolgirls, lamplighters, the gondoliers of Venice, and people who suffer from hemorrhages. Syracuse, Sicily, was St. Lucy's hometown and the site of her martyrdom. She was scarcely older than a schoolgirl when she died for the Christian faith. In the days before electricity, men on foot, horseback, or bicycle each evening would hurry from lamppost to lamppost in cities and light the oil or gas lamps with the flaming torch they carried. In Venice, Italy, the gondoliers often sing the song "Santa Lucia" as they guide their gondolas, lit by lamps at night, up and down the canals of that city. And finally, Lucy's mother Eutychia was cured of a hemorrhage problem, so people who have similar illnesses call upon Lucy to pray for them.

No one is certain where St. Lucy is buried. The Venetians claim, however, that she is buried in the Church of San Geremia, which is near that city's Santa Lucia Railroad Station, named in her honor. The Venetians say that after St. Lucy's martyrdom in Syracuse her bones were taken to Constantinople in 1038, and then knights on a crusade brought them to Venice in 1204. Another story, however, tells that St. Lucy's bones traveled from Syracuse to Abruzzo, Italy, and finally in 969 to Metz, France, where they were reburied.

Sometimes this martyr is known as St. Lucy of Syracuse.

St. Valentine

On St. Valentine's Day, February 14, children exchange colorful cards with their schoolmates. Dads bring home presents—perhaps heart-shaped boxes of chocolates or red roses—for the girls in the family, especially for the moms. Young men in love spend their spare dollars on special gifts for their sweethearts. These customs, however, have little to do with a saint named Valentine.

The gift-giving on February 14 dates back many centuries to customs of the Romans, the English, the French, and the Italians. About two thousand years ago, the Romans honored the goddess Februato Juno, the wife of Jupiter, the king of the gods, on February 15. To this queen of the gods, the Roman women brought gifts and prayed, particularly on this day, for the blessing of many children. In the late fifth century, Pope St. Gelasius I, in reaction to this pagan festival, replaced it with two Christian feast days, February 14, St. Valentine's Day, and February 15, the Feast of the Purification of the Virgin.

St. Valentine

b. ?

d. February 14, 269

Feast Day — formerly on February 14

Meaning of name — strong, healthy, from the Latin *valere*

Latin
Valentinus

Spanish
Valentín

Italian
Valentino

Portuguese
Valentim

German, French, Norwegian
Valentin

English
Valentine
Val
Valentina f.

Some centuries later in England, France, and Italy, February 14 was a day on which lovers sent gifts and greetings to one another. That supposedly was the day in late winter when the birds began to pair, build their nests, and start raising a family. The poet Chaucer in England during the fourteenth century wrote that "on St. Valentine's Day, every fowl comes to choose its mate." It became customary on that day for people to send greetings or gifts to someone they loved or to call that boy or girl, man or woman, their "Valentine." Thus, the saint by that name became the protector of that day and that still-popular custom.

During the early centuries of the Church, Valentine was a popular name, much like the names John, Michael, or James are popular today. The Church lists several Valentines in its register of saints. Some

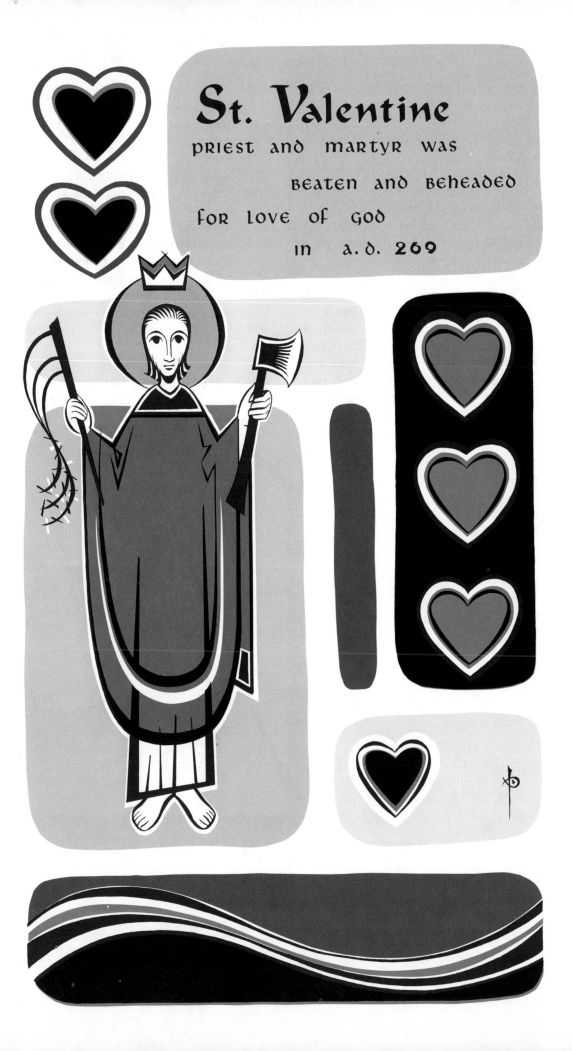

St. Valentine

priest and martyr was

beaten and beheaded

for love of god

in a.d. 269

were martyrs who died cruel deaths for their Christian beliefs. Several were priests, three were bishops, and another was Pope St. Valentine, who reigned for only forty days in the year 827.

The saint usually associated with the name Valentine was a Roman nobleman and a pagan priest who eventually became a Christian. Each day he would visit the dungeons in Rome where the Christians were awaiting martyrdom. For a while the soldiers did not suspect Valentine of being a Christian, since he was of noble birth. After some time, however, the guards became suspicious of this good man who faithfully visited their prisoners and encouraged them to be strong as they awaited execution. To test him, the soldiers stopped Valentine and ordered him to worship some statues of the Roman gods.

When Valentine refused, they arrested him and in time imposed the punishment ordered by Emperor Claudius II—death. The date was February 14, 269.

Another St. Valentine, also a martyr, was the bishop of Terni, a city about sixty miles from Rome. It may be that this Valentine was the one and the same person as the other saint, but was brought from Terni to Rome for his martyrdom. It is clear, however, that the Christians of that time, both in Rome and in Terni, honored the memory of a St. Valentine. A catacomb or hiding place for the early Christians, a church, and even a gate of the city, Porto Valentini in Rome, were named in his honor.

The Church no longer assigns a specific feast day to the Sts. Valentine.

St. Thomas More

Thomas More wrote that he came from a family "not famous but of honest stock." It was his honesty that four hundred years ago made Thomas the most important person, except for the king himself, in all of England. It was his honesty and his wish to follow his conscience and God that led Thomas to sainthood. Because Sir Thomas More, a knight and King Henry VIII's lord chancellor, would not disobey his conscience, the king ordered his execution.

All of Europe mourned Sir Thomas' death in 1535. Many biographies written during that century and in later times tell this nobleman's heroic story. In recent years, for example, *A Man for All Seasons*, a play by Robert Bolt, has been seen on stage and screen by millions. The sir who became a saint is a man to be remembered.

Thomas grew up in London, the thriving capital of merry England. Since he came from a family of lawyers, his parents encouraged him to study law. At age thirteen his father sent him to be a page in the house of the lord chancellor, the chief judge of the realm. Little did Thomas know that forty years later he himself would serve England and the next king in that distinguished position.

Thomas went on to Oxford University for two years and then returned to London to study law. In 1501 he was admitted to the bar, which meant that as a lawyer he could argue cases in court. But it was four years before Thomas entered a courtroom to try a case. He spent that time in a monastery, finding out firsthand how monks worshiped and worked. God, however, did not plan that Thomas should become a monk.

In 1504 Thomas married a prominent woman named Lady Jane Colt and that same year was elected to Parliament, the lawmaking body of England. An able lawyer, Thomas earned a good living. He worked both for the rich and the poor. One day he would meet with

---

St. Thomas More

b. February 7, 1477

d. July 6, 1535

Feast Day — June 22

Meaning of name — twin, from the Aramaic *tĕ'öma*

Latin, French	Norwegian
Thomas	**Tomas**
Spanish	*English*
Tomás	**Thomas**
Tomasa f.	**Tom**
Italian	**Thom**
Tommaso	**Tommy**
	Maso
Portuguese	**Thomasa**
Thomas	**Thomasine** ⌐f.
Thomaz	**Tami**
German	**Tammy**
Thomas	**Tanzine**

ST. THOMAS MORE

the king's ambassadors to settle some government problem, and the next day he would defend poor people in court, pleading their cases at no charge.

Six happy years passed, but then his wife Jane died, leaving Thomas alone to raise their four young children. He realized that his children should have a foster mother, so he soon married a lady who was seven years older than himself. Thomas said that Dame Alice was "neither a pearl nor a girl," but he grew to love her dearly, and she took good care of him and his children.

At his home called Great House at Chelsea near London, Sir Thomas lived simply and prayerfully, even wearing a hair shirt next to his skin for penance. Often poor families were guests at meals in Great House. In 1521 Thomas, now a counselor to the king, was knighted, thereby gaining the title "Sir." Two years later he was elected as the speaker or leader in Parliament. Sir Thomas, an expert on literature as well as law, wrote several books, including his famous *Utopia,* which described how people should live in happiness in an ideal community. He was respected at home in England and in other European countries.

The king, unlike Sir Thomas, was an unhappy man. He wanted to divorce his wife, a Spanish princess named Catherine, and marry another woman. But King Henry knew that the laws of God and of his Church clearly taught that no man could marry a second time as long as his first wife lived. Not even a king could do that. King Henry then dismissed his chancellor, Cardinal Wolsey, who could not help him divorce Queen Catherine. The king then appointed Sir Thomas, a layman, as the next chancellor.

For two and a half years Sir Thomas as chancellor ruled justly and promptly on more than four thousand legal cases. The king thought that he would eventually take his side on the divorce matter, but not so. On May 15, 1532, most of the important officials in England, including all but one bishop, agreed with the king about his right to divorce Queen Catherine. But Sir Thomas did not. Rather than disobey his conscience and

obey his king, Sir Thomas resigned as the lord chancellor.

For a year Sir Thomas lived quietly at Chelsea, no longer practicing law, no longer a wealthy man, since he had lost his royal salary. The king did not forget Thomas' defiance of him, especially when Sir Thomas did not attend the coronation of Anne Boleyn, King Henry's second wife and queen.

The next chancellor, an evil man named Thomas Cromwell, plotted against Sir Thomas. He had him arrested and brought to the famous Tower of London. For fifteen months Sir Thomas was imprisoned because he would not approve the divorce nor would he sign a paper saying that King Henry was the head of the Church in England. Then Cromwell convinced another rogue, Sir Richard Roth, to lie about Sir Thomas at his trial. Sir Thomas was then convicted on false charges of treason or treachery to the king. The sentence was death.

After the verdict was read and the sentence pronounced, Sir Thomas gave a magnificent speech to the bishops, lords, and knights present at his trial in Westminster Hall where the Parliament met. He told them quite plainly that all the councils of the Christian world would support him in the decision of his conscience. On his way back to the Tower, he said good-bye to his eldest daughter Margaret and her husband William Roper. With his last letter to her, he sent his hair shirt.

On the morning of July 6, 1535, Sir Thomas walked calmly to the place of his death at Tower Hill near the prison. His former friend and king had decreed a less painful execution for him—death by beheading rather than by being hanged, drawn, and quartered. To the anxious crowd of spectators who waited at the scaffold, Sir Thomas remarked most seriously that he would die "the king's good servant, but God's first." Then, after reciting a prayer, he turned to the nervous executioner, put a gold coin in his hand, and said jokingly, "Courage, my good man, don't be afraid, but take care, for I have a short neck and you have to look to your honor." Finally, Sir Thomas, after placing the blindfold over his eyes himself, knelt down and put his head on the block—carefully moving his beard out of the way, which, he said, "did not deserve to be cut off since it had betrayed nothing." Then he took the blow of the axe.

Sir Thomas was buried in the chapel of the Tower. Following the custom after an execution, the officials placed his head on London Bridge as a warning to all passers-by that strict punishment awaited anyone who committed a capital crime. A few days earlier Bishop John Fisher, the only bishop who, like Sir Thomas, would not agree to the king's divorce, had likewise been executed. Today Sir Thomas' head rests in the Roper family vault in St. Dunstan's Church near Canterbury in southeast England. The famous hair shirt is preserved in a convent in Devonshire in western England.

In 1935, four hundred years after their deaths, Pope Pius XI canonized Bishop John Fisher and Sir Thomas More. The Pope called Sir Thomas "the martyr of the papacy." Like the popes, Sir Thomas and Bishop Fisher defended the Church's belief that Christian marriage demands a lifelong commitment of husband and wife.

St. Thomas More is the patron of lawyers and university students.

North American Martyrs

In the early 1600s upstate New York and the provinces of Quebec and Ontario in Canada were wilderness country that only the Indians called home. Emigrants from the Old World were just beginning to settle New England and New France. After explorers mapped this territory, French and English settlers came to farm the land, to harvest the timber, and to hunt and trap the wildlife for furs and pelts. With the settlers came missionaries to build and to staff churches and schools and to preach the Word of God to the homesteaders and the Indians.

North American Martyrs	
Isaac Jogues —	b. January 10, 1607
	d. October 18, 1646
Antoine Daniel —	b. May 27, 1601
	d. July 4, 1648
Jean de Brébeuf —	b. March 25, 1593
	d. March 16, 1649
Gabriel Lalemant —	b. October 10, 1610
	d. March 17, 1649
Charles Garnier —	b. about 1605
	d. December 7, 1649
Noël Chabanel —	b. February 7, 1613
	d. December 8, 1649
René Goupil —	b. May 13, 1608
	d. September 29, 1642
Jean de la Lande —	b. ?
	d. October 19, 1646
Feast Day —	October 19

The twenty thousand Hurons who had settled along the eastern shore of Lake Huron did not always welcome the settlers. Too often they were forced to give up their hunting grounds to the newcomers, who took the best lands for towns and farms. It was not easy for the Indians to accept the white man's religion. To the black-robed Jesuits they put questions like "Do you hunt in heaven, or make war, or go to a feast?" "No," they were told. "Then we won't go; it isn't good to be lazy."

Sometimes the Hurons blamed the priests' crosses, rosaries, medals, and other belongings for bringing bad luck, poor crops, a shortage of game, or an epidemic of smallpox. It took the Hurons many moons to accept the Jesuits as friends. Theirs was a new religion, taught by strangers from the other side of the Atlantic. They had reasons to be suspicious.

By the 1640s the Jesuits had lived and worked with the Hurons long enough to develop a mutual trust. The Huron nations were beginning to accept Christianity. They found Jesuit priests like Isaac Jogues, Antoine Daniel, Jean de Brébeuf, Gabriel Lalemant, Charles Garnier, and Noël Chabanel, as well as their helpers René Goupil and Jean de la Lande, to be men they could trust. These missionaries

STS. ISAAC JOGUES, JOHN DE BRÉBEUF AND COMPANIONS – MARTYRS

helped them with their day-to-day tasks and brought them medicine when they were sick. Father Jogues could even outrun the fastest braves in a race. Many Hurons chose to worship the God of the missionaries.

During these years the Hurons often had deadly skirmishes with their mortal enemies to the southeast, the Iroquois. This Indian nation had no time for the Hurons and anyone who worked with them, including the Jesuits. Between September 29, 1642, and December 8, 1649, seven of these missionaries were murdered, either by the Iroquois or by the Mohawks. Today the Church remembers these French missionaries as the North American Martyrs.

René Goupil, a *donne* or helper to the Jesuit priests, was the first to be martyred. René truly lived the meaning of the French verb *donner*, which means ''to give.'' He gave his life in the service of the Lord. In France he had studied surgery before coming to Huronia about 1640. Both the missionaries and their Indian converts called on René's talents to nurse them back to health, especially in the long, cold winters when there was much sickness. (Today St. René Goupil is remembered as the patron of anesthetists, those trained to administer drugs which put patients to sleep during surgery.)

On one journey René and Father Jogues were captured by Iroquois. Back at their camp, the Indians cruelly tortured them. Their hair, beards, and nails were torn off. They were beaten with sticks and had their fingers bitten through. When René made the Sign of the Cross over a child, an Iroquois brave punished him with a tomahawk blow which took his life. Somehow Father Jogues survived that day, which was September 29, 1642.

Some months passed before Father Jogues was ransomed by the Dutch. Eventually he made his way to New York and then across the Atlantic to France, but just for a visit. Father Jogues was determined to return to Huronia. Pope Urban VIII heard about his dedication as a missionary and gave him permission to say Mass even though his fingers had been mutilated in that torture. The Pope said that ''it would be shameful for a martyr of Christ not to drink the Blood of Christ.''

It did not take long for Father Jogues to return to Huronia. One of the first things he did was to help the Hurons make a peace treaty with the Iroquois. But, in September 1646, on a journey to establish a mission with the Mohawks, he and his helper Jean de la Lande were captured by an angry Mohawk war party. That October 18, when Father Jogues stooped to enter the long house of the chief, who had invited him to a meeting, he was tomahawked to death. A similar execution awaited Jean the next day.

Fr. Antoine Daniel was the parish priest at the Huron town of St. Joseph. On the morning of July 4, 1648, just after he had celebrated Mass, Iroquois war parties surprised the town. Father Daniel told the Hurons near him to flee if they could, telling them, ''I will stay here. We shall meet in heaven.'' Still wearing Mass vestments, Father Daniel ministered to the wounded, baptizing some of them, but the Iroquois were too powerful. The mission fell. Both arrows and bullets struck Father Daniel. The Iroquois then trampled his body underfoot and tossed it into the fire which consumed the chapel.

An even worse fate, if that can be imagined, overtook Fr. Jean de Brébeuf and Fr. Gabriel Lalemant. They were captured by an Iroquois band which attacked the town of Ignace on March 16, 1649. The priests were tied to stakes and tortured to death by fire, red-hot stones, and boiling water.

After thirteen years in Huronia, Fr. Charles Garnier had adapted well to the tough life which the Indians and the missionaries faced daily. He could tolerate the unwholesome aspects of wilderness living— cold, heat, smoke, hunger, and sickness. Entire families lived in one-room lodges, along with their dogs, inhaling smoke from a winter's fire that over a long period caused sickness, even blindness. Father Garnier learned to survive a famine by eating roots and acorns. He would gladly walk forty miles in the summer's heat to baptize a dying Indian. On December 7, 1649, a martyr's death came to this missionary. The Iroquois surprised the mission at St. Ignace, and Father Garnier was struck by two bullets and then tomahawked.

Fr. Noël Chabanel died at the hands of a Huron, who killed the priest in hatred for having been converted a Christian. The Huron later admitted that he blamed the missionaries for the hard times that his family experienced. Father Chabanel did not particularly care for the missionary life in New France. More than once he remembered the easier duties he had in France, where he was a brilliant professor of composition. But his dislike of missionary work only convinced him to promise God that he would continue to preach the gospel of Jesus until the end of his life. He died a martyr on December 8, 1649.

The North American Martyrs were canonized saints of the Church in 1930. Today thousands of pilgrims each year visit shrines to their memory at Auriesville, New York, and Midland, Ontario.

St. Maximilian Kolbe

At the beatification of Blessed Maximilian Kolbe in October, 1971, a white-haired gentleman with tears in his eyes led the procession with the gifts to the main altar of St. Peter's Basilica, and there, sobbing in gratitude, embraced Pope Paul VI.

On a hot July evening thirty years earlier, this man, Sergeant Franciszek Gajowniczek of the Polish Army, watched in horror as the angry commandant of the Nazi concentration camp of Auschwitz in southwest Poland walked their ranks and selected at random ten inmates to be executed. The reason: two days earlier a prisoner was thought to have escaped Block 14 of that dreaded camp (actually the poor fellow had drowned in a latrine and disappeared from sight). Some of the condemned cursed their jailers; others praised Poland; still others broke down. Sergeant Gajowniczek wept uncontrollably: "My poor wife, my poor children."

> **St. Maximilian Kolbe**
>
> *b.* **January 8, 1894**
>
> *d.* **August 14, 1941**
>
> **Founder of the Knights of the Immaculate One**
>
> **Feast Day—October 10**
>
> **Meaning of name—great or famous, from the Latin *maximus***
>
> *German, Polish*
> Maximilian
>
> *English*
> Maximilian
> Max
> Maxi
> Maxey
> Maxwell
> Maxim

Witnessing that shock and grief, a 47-year-old inmate (number 16670), dressed in the striped uniform of the camp, immediately stepped out of the formation and volunteered to take the sergeant's place. When the commandant, utterly amazed by this action, asked who he was, the man answered, "I am a Catholic priest." His offer was accepted, and the sergeant and the priest changed places. With that, Fr. Maximilian Kolbe and the other victims of that fatal order were placed in a basement cell, where they were left to die of hunger, thirst, and neglect.

Months of forced labor, meager food, and abuse had all but exhausted the inmates' bodies long before this sentencing. Years earlier Father Kolbe's health was ravaged by tuberculosis, leaving him with only one functioning lung. Now, in the death cell, the ten prepared to die, turning to Father Kolbe's leadership in prayer and song. Slowly the doomed men slipped into unconsciousness, and one by one they died. After two weeks, only four, including Father Kolbe, were still alive. At that point, since this dingy space was needed for other in-

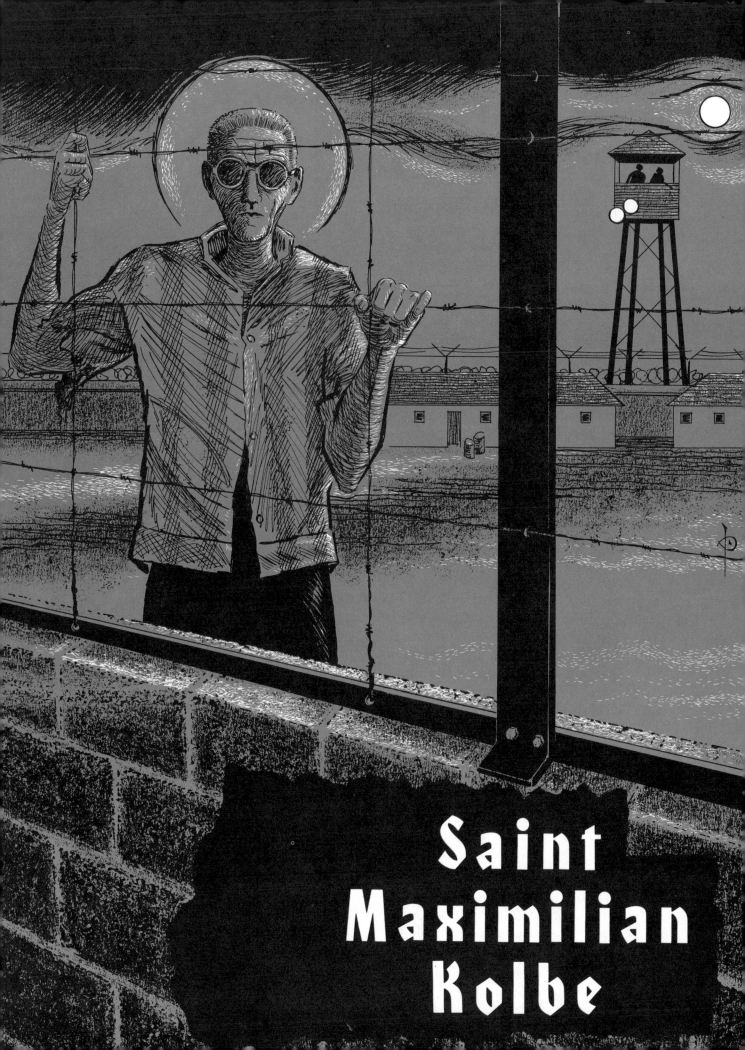

Saint
Maximilian
Kolbe

mates similarly sentenced, the camp doctor injected carbolic acid into their veins. At sunset that evening, August 14, Father Kolbe died. The next day, his body—like the five million inmates who did not survive Auschwitz and World War II—was incinerated in a furnace built by inmate labor.

Bruno Borgowiec, who escaped this holocaust because the Nazis needed him as an interpreter, was an eyewitness to Father Kolbe's last days: "From the cell where those unfortunates were buried alive, you could hear every day prayers recited aloud, the Rosary and hymns. . . . Sometimes they would be so absorbed in prayer that they would not even realize that the guards had entered for daily inspection. . . . Father Maximilian would greet us either standing or kneeling with a look of serenity on his face."

It is significant that Father Kolbe died on August 14, the eve of the Feast of the Assumption of Mary. He had been particularly devoted to the Blessed Mother. Through her, he taught, many are introduced to her Son Jesus, the Savior. In 1917, a year before being ordained a priest, he and six other Franciscans founded the *Militia Immaculatae* or "Army of the Immaculate One," an organization dedicated to advancing devotion to Mary, the Mother of God. Upon finishing his seminary studies in Rome and returning to his native Poland as a young priest, Father Kolbe started a magazine to tell of the work of these soldiers of Mary.

That work was most successful. By 1938 over a million copies of *The Knight of the Immaculate* circulated among the Polish people and elsewhere. Eventually the Knights numbered more than two million members in several countries. Also by 1938 nearly eight hundred Franciscan brothers, priests, and seminarians lived with Father Kolbe at a settlement near Warsaw called *Niepokalanow* (the City of the Immaculate). It became the largest community of Franciscan men in the world. In 1927 Father Kolbe had established this self-supporting community as a center for religious life and apostolates such as publishing and radio broadcasting. Three years later he founded a similar center in

Nagasaki, Japan. Sheltered by a hill, this settlement, called the Garden of the Immaculate, survived the atomic bomb blast of 1945. In the United States Franciscan friars have founded a "Marytown" in Libertyville, Illinois.

When Poland fell to the Nazi tank divisions in 1939, Father Kolbe was the head of an important publishing complex of religious magazines and newspapers. The German tyrants knew that in order to break the will of the Poles they had to arrest, imprison, and even murder thousands of the professional, political, and religious leaders of that nation. If the Catholic press could be silenced, the Nazi goal of total control of the Polish people, for centuries loyal to the Church, would be easier to reach.

That September the German secret police, the Gestapo, arrested the superior of the Warsaw *Niepokalanow* and charged him with aiding Jewish refugees and the Polish resistance. Indeed, this community, despite surveillance by the Nazis, sheltered some two thousand refugees. The Nazis feared that the printing presses of the Knights might be used by the Polish underground. Father Kolbe was first deported to Lamsdorf in Germany and then to the concentration camp at Amtitz. But, on December 8, the Feast of Mary's Immaculate Conception, the Germans released him.

More than a year passed before the authorities in February, 1941, arrested Father Kolbe a second time. He was kept in Warsaw's notorious Pawiak Prison before being moved to Auschwitz that May, where three months later he was martyred.

As a Capuchin friar (a branch of the Franciscan Order), priest, journalist, and skilled administrator, Father Kolbe taught and lived the Good News from day to day, as did St. Francis of Assisi. Finally, by offering his life so that another could live, Father Kolbe gave himself completely to Jesus, who told us that "there is no greater love than this: to lay down one's life for one's friends" (John 15:13).

Long before that dreadful day in July, 1941, the inmates, and even the guards, were well aware of Father Kolbe's constant heroic action. He was the counselor who encouraged them not to abandon hope, despite beatings, slave labor, and the miserable routine of the concentration camp. He was the priest who risked punishment to hear their confessions. He was the brown-robed friar who at the Pawiak Prison calmly answered over and over again, "Yes, I believe in this," while a German officer in a rage repeatedly slapped his face and tore the crucifix from the Rosary on Father Kolbe's belt. He was the inmate who was always last, even in a line of hundreds, to seek treatment from an inmate doctor at the camp hospital. He was the Good Samaritan who often shared his meager ration of bread with someone more hungry. To a guard who treated him with special cruelty, he was the long-suffering Christian who replied, "May God forgive you."

The world that survived World War II soon recognized this courage and love. In 1947 the Church ordered that the cause for sainthood for Fr. Maximilian Kolbe be officially investigated. Reports of miracles through the intercession of Father Kolbe, the "Martyr of Auschwitz," reached the Vatican. When two such cures had been certified, he was beatified by Pope Paul VI in 1971 and given the title "confessor," a holy person who professes the beliefs of Catholicism in an outstanding way.

Eleven years later, on October 10, 1982, more than one hundred and fifty thousand people—including some ten thousand Poles—crowded into St. Peter's Square to witness the canonization of Father Kolbe. Among them was Angela Testoni, an Italian woman from Sardinia who had been cured of pulmonary tuberculosis through Father Kolbe's intercession. There, Pope John Paul II, who both as a cardinal and as Pope had visited Auschwitz, wearing the red vestments that symbolize martyrdom, proclaimed Blessed Maximilian a saint and martyr of the Church. What joy Pope John Paul must have felt in knowing that the first canonization of his pontificate was that of a fellow Pole!

Among the pilgrims to Rome for the canonization was Franciszek Gajowniczek, age 81—the man whose death sentence was served by St. Maximilian Kolbe.

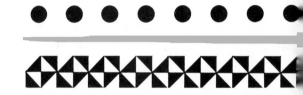

5. Bishops

St. Patrick

In Ireland it is a rare family that has not named a son or daughter Patrick or Patricia, honoring the bishop-saint who fifteen hundred years ago converted the Irish to Christianity. Patrick, the "Apostle of Ireland," was born in Wales, which is just across the Irish Sea from Ireland. Patrick was the son of a Roman *decurion* or alderman named Calpornius. Wales was then part of the Roman Empire. At age sixteen Patricius, which was his Roman name, was kidnapped by pirates and brought to Ireland. There for six years Patricius was a slave to a chieftain named Milchu.

Patrick had a tough life under Milchu, tending his flocks as a shepherd, scarcely having enough to eat. He was often cold and almost always by himself. In his solitude he came to know God. "The love of God came to me more and more, and my faith was strengthened," he said.

Patrick used his spare time well, learning the Irish language and praying daily for a chance to escape. One day when Patrick was twenty-two that opportunity came. Patrick fled Milchu's grasp and walked two hundred miles through strange country before he reached the seacoast. Three months later, after several perilous adventures, Patrick arrived in England and eventually found the home of some relatives.

Though he was now safe in England, Patrick wanted someday to return to Ireland to convert the Irish people to Christianity. Most of the Irish then followed a pagan religion called Druidism. To prepare to become the Apostle of Ireland, as he is known today, Patrick studied to be a priest, either in England or France.

Some years later Pope Celestine I asked Patrick to preach the Word of God to the Irish. Patrick was only too happy to say yes to the Pope's request. Thus, in the year 433, Patrick, now a bishop, returned with a few companions to Ireland. Since he spoke Irish and knew the

St. Patrick

b. about 389

d. 461

Apostle of Ireland

Feast Day — March 17

Meaning of name — of noble birth, from the Latin *patricius*

French	*Norwegian, Latin*
Patrice	**Patricius**
Spanish, Portuguese	*English*
Patricio	**Patrick**
Italian	**Paddy**
Patrizio	**Partridge**
	Rick
German	**Pat** — m., f.
Patrizius	**Patsy**
Irish	**Patty**
	Patricia
Pádraig	**Trish** f.
Scottish	**Tricia**
Pate	

ST.
PATRICK

customs of the people, Patrick's sermons soon attracted crowds who listened with interest to the Good News of Jesus. Some Druid priests and their followers, however, tried to drive Patrick from that Emerald Isle.

On Easter Sunday that year at Tara, north of Dublin, Patrick spoke to a huge assembly about Jesus and his gospel. That day the people saw proof that Patrick could defy the Druid gods without being harmed. Patrick convinced the chieftains and Druid priests of that part of Ireland that Christianity was the true religion. It is said that at Tara Patrick picked up a clover-like plant called a shamrock from the grass and used it to explain the Trinity—three persons, Father, Son, and Holy Spirit who are united in one God. Today the shamrock, which some say grows only in Ireland, is a symbol of that country and the Irish people.

After his success at Tara, for many years Patrick crisscrossed the green hills and valleys of Ireland, preaching the gospel. Within twenty-five years Ireland was a Christian country. Patrick first converted the chieftains of the many little kingdoms in Ireland. They in turn would convince their subjects to be baptized.

When Patrick came to Ireland as a bishop in 433, Christianity was scarcely known in that country. When he died about the year 461, almost thirty years later, Ireland was a land dotted with churches attended by a deeply religious people. The Irish have provided the Church through the centuries since Patrick with thousands of priests, sisters, and brothers. Even today Ireland sends many priests and religious as missionaries to distant countries, including the United States. There they tell the Good News of Jesus as Patrick did to the Irish.

In Ireland St. Patrick's feast day on March 17 is a holy day like a Sunday, as well as a national holiday. Families wear their best clothes, sporting fresh shamrocks in their lapels, and attend Mass. After church the women go home to cook a festive dinner and the men gather at a pub. One custom there is to order a drink called a "half-one" and then to "drown the shamrock" in it. At the noon meal an Irish family would probably eat baked salmon, Dublin bay prawns, or some other special dish. It is a day of dancing the reel and the jig, of visiting friends and relatives, a day of no school or work, of remembering the heritage of Ireland.

In Irish-American cities such as Boston, New York, and St. Paul, there is plenty of celebration on St. Patrick's Day too, but much of it is what the Irish call "shamrockery." The "Kiss me, I'm Irish" buttons, the green beer and milkshakes, the Irish vs. everyone else tugs-of-war on college campuses, and the elaborate parades are customs more American than Irish in origin. In Chicago, part of the celebration, led by the mayor, might include turning the Chicago River green with hundreds of pounds of dye. In San Francisco youngsters race snakes around a bright green track, calling attention to the myth that St. Patrick chased the snakes out of Ireland.

The Irish, however, do add a bit to this shamrockery. Aer Lingus International Airlines jets fresh shamrocks to some American cities on March 17. Irish celebrities lead parades down Fifth Avenue in New York and in other cities. Like the Irish, the Irish-Americans often attend Mass on St. Patrick's Day. Special Masses are celebrated in St. Patrick's Cathedral in New York, where a relic of the saint is enshrined in the main altar, and elsewhere. St. Patrick is a much celebrated saint.

St. Stanislaus

On the main altar of the cathedral in the city of Cracow, Poland, rests a burial casket that is held in place by silver angels or cherubim. The casket contains the bones of a famous saint of Poland. This saint, Stanislaus, is the patron of the cathedral, the city of Cracow, and all of Poland.

Stanislaus Szczepanowski was born in 1030 of noble parents in Szczepanow, Poland. His parents sent their son to the best schools, first to the cathedral school at Griezno—then the capital of Poland—and later to Paris, France.

Stanislaus decided as a young man to be a priest. After he had completed his studies, he was ordained by the bishop of Cracow, Lambert Zula. The bishop assigned him as a canon or priest of the cathedral parish. There Stanislaus soon became known as a brilliant preacher. Churchgoers came from the far corners of this large city to hear him preach on Sundays.

St. Stanislaus

b. **July 26, 1030**
d. **April 11, 1079**

Patron of Poland

Feast Day — April 11

Meaning of name — camp glory

French	*English*
Stanislas	**Stanislaus**
Italian	
Stanislao	
Portuguese	
Estanislau	
German, Polish	
Stanislav	

When Bishop Zula died, Father Szczepanowski was a likely candidate to succeed him as the next bishop of Cracow. It was no surprise in 1072 when Pope Alexander II appointed him to that position. Bishop Szczepanowski grew to be loved by the people of Cracow. They knew that he was interested in every aspect of their welfare—jobs, food, homes, friendship, and spiritual help. The bishop's house was often crowded with the poor who came to him for a meal, a place to stay, or some kindly advice.

Poland was beset with many problems that bothered Stanislaus, and he was not afraid to speak out and to try to correct them. He even raised his voice against the king, a cruel man named Boleslaus II. The king was so mean that his subjects called him Boleslaus the Cruel. One day the king carried off the wife of one of his noblemen. The bishop then boldly told Boleslaus that he could no longer be a member of the Church if he did not return that woman to her husband.

The other Polish bishops were afraid to criticize the king, but not Stanislaus. He knew that a king should know right from wrong and, if he pretended not to, he should be corrected. King Boleslaus did not take kindly to this reprimand and tried to ruin the bishop's reputation by spreading false stories. But this mean gossip fell on deaf ears. The people of Cracow had plenty of proof that their bishop was a good man.

Boleslaus was not angry at Stanislaus only for criticizing him face-to-face in public. The king was upset also because Stanislaus had joined the forces of the king's brother Ladislaus against him. The king had just fought a long and expensive war against the Grand Duchy of Kiev. Many Polish citizens sided with Ladislaus against the king; they saw no reason to continue the endless fighting and suffering. Because of this, Boleslaus considered the bishop a traitor and sentenced him to death.

Meanwhile, since Boleslaus would not change his ways, the bishop announced that the king could no longer receive the sacraments. Upon hearing this, Boleslaus, raging mad, rushed to the cathedral looking for the bishop. But the huge church was empty because public services were not held during the period of the king's excommunication. Boleslaus nevertheless kept searching for the bishop, intending to impose the sentence of execution by having swordsmen hack his body to pieces.

It wasn't long before the king found Stanislaus at the Chapel of St. Michael just outside Cracow, where the bishop was celebrating Mass. The furious Boleslaus ordered his soldiers to murder the bishop. But when they approached Stanislaus the soldiers were turned back by a bright heavenly light that surrounded Stanislaus. Disgusted with their timidity, the king himself rushed into the chapel and killed the bishop, splitting his head open with his sword. Boleslaus the Cruel, true to his name, next ordered the soldiers to cut up the bishop's body. It was then scattered about the grounds of the chapel to be left for stray animals to eat. The soldiers and King Boleslaus then left the scene of the murder.

Three days later, when it was safe, the priests of the cathedral came to the Chapel of St. Michael to pick up the remains of their bishop. They found that the animals had not touched them. Eagles, it is said, protected the holy bishop's mutilated body until the priests came. The priests then buried their bishop at the door of the chapel.

When Pope Gregory VII heard about that vile murder, he placed Poland under an interdict. That meant that for a time the people could not receive the sacraments. All those who assisted the king in the murder were also excommunicated. Boleslaus now realized that he could never defeat his own people who strongly favored his brother. Thus he fled to Hungary where he had relatives among the royalty. In time Boleslaus repented for his evil deeds and spent his later years at the Benedictine abbey of Osiak.

In the year 1088, eleven years after Stanislaus was martyred, Lambert III, his successor as the bishop of Cracow, brought the remains of Stanislaus to the cathedral. He placed them in the silver casket that now rests on the altar. Bishop Lambert then renamed the cathedral in honor of Stanislaus.

In 1253, in Assisi, Italy, Pope Innocent IV canonized Stanislaus a saint.

ST. STANISLAUS

St. Augustine of Hippo

St. Augustine is often pictured holding a burning heart in his hand. Indeed such a symbol is most appropriate. As a young man whose main interest was pleasure, his heart often burned with disgust and disappointment because he could not make up his mind to live a good life. "I longed to give up my sinful life," he said, "but I was bound tightly, not with exterior chains but with my own iron will." Not until he was thirty-two did Augustine resolve to live as a Christian. From then on, until his death forty-four years later, Augustine's heart burned with a desire to serve God and his neighbor.

Augustine lived sixteen centuries ago in what is now Algeria in North Africa. Augustine had a rather unhappy childhood that led to a delinquent youth. He hated school, fell in with bad companions, all but ignored his parents' directives, especially that of his good and holy mother, St. Monica. For Augustine the only thing that mattered much was having a good time, going to one party after the other, spending every free moment in theaters, sports arenas, bars, and restaurants in and around Tagaste, his hometown. Playing tricks on people, telling lies, cheating, and stealing were common to his lifestyle.

When he put his mind to it, however, Augustine did well in his studies. He was especially sharp at speech and writing, what was then called rhetoric. Later, as a teacher, he opened his own schools in Tagaste and Carthage. When in time he decided to leave North Africa, he crossed the Mediterranean to Rome, Italy, and started a school in

St. Augustine of Hippo

b. November 13, 354

d. August 28, 430

Doctor of the Church

Feast Day — August 28

Meaning of name — belonging to Augustus, from the Latin *Augustinus*

French
Augustin
Augustine f.

Spanish
Agustín

Italian
Agostino

German
Augustine
Auguste f.

(Austrian)
Gustl
Gusti f.

Norwegian
Augustan

English
Augustine
August
Austin
Augie
Gus
Augusta
Gussie f.

that huge city. That adventure did not work out for Augustine. He found that life in Rome was difficult for a foreigner. His students cheated him out of tuition. He was poor, lonely, and often sick.

One day Augustine won a contest that awarded him an important teaching position in Milan. That city was then the center of the Roman government and the court of the emperor. There he was soon recognized as a brilliant teacher and was invited to speak before the emperor's court. Unfortunately, the ideas that Augustine believed and taught were in part untrue and misguided. At that time Augustine was a Manichean, one who believed that the forces of good and evil are of equal power and battle each other for victory.

His patient mother, Monica, never gave up praying and hoping that her son would reform his lifestyle and change his mind about Manicheism. Fortunately, in Milan, Augustine met a famous preacher, a bishop named Ambrose. The more he listened to the bishop and the more he read the Bible, the more Augustine wanted to make the break with his reckless ways; but something still held him back.

One September day in 386, however, Augustine found the courage to make the most important decision of his life—to follow Jesus. This happened while he and his friend Alipius were talking to a man named Pontitian. He told them about two courtiers who had suddenly been converted to God's service after reading the life of Antony the Hermit. As Pontitian described St. Antony's life, Augustine's soul began to stir.

After Pontitian left, Augustine and Alipius stepped into a nearby garden and sat down to think at a spot some distance from the house. His heart full of inner conflict, Augustine then moved further into the garden. He prayed, "How long, O Lord!"—how long before his soul would find peace. Then, while in this state of wonder and prayer, Augustine heard some children at play outside the garden say, "Take up and read."

With that message bouncing around in his mind, Augustine hurried back to Alipius, who was then reading a book of St. Paul's Letters. Augustine reached for this book and without hesitation opened it and read the first lines to meet his eyes. The passage told him: "Let us conduct ourselves properly, as people who live in the light of day—no orgies or drunkenness, no immorality or indecency, no fighting or jealousy. But take up the weapons of the Lord Jesus Christ, and stop paying attention to your sinful nature and satisfying its desires" (Romans 13:13-14).

The message was strong and clear—follow Jesus. Augustine's life changed dramatically. Before long he moved to the country outside Milan, where with Monica, his brother Navigias, his son Adeodatus, Alipius, and other friends, he began a life of prayer and service. That next year, 387, on Holy Saturday evening, St. Ambrose baptized Augustine, Alipius, and Adeodatus.

Eventually Augustine returned to North Africa and to his family's home in Tagaste, where quietly and prayerfully for about the next three years he lived with friends, spending his time studying and performing good works. Before long Bishop Valerius of Hippo, hearing of Augustine's talent for preaching and his love of God, called upon him to serve the Church as a priest. In time Augustine became Valerius' assistant, and after the bishop died, Augustine succeeded him as the chief pastor of this important ancient city.

Bishop Augustine insisted that the priests and workers in his house and office live simply as did monks. Except for spoons, they had no silver on their dining room table. Plain food was served on wood and clay dishes. Often while eating they listened to a reading from the Bible rather than chitchat about the news in town that day. They all wore similar clothing, which was simple and practical. Spare money went to the poor. They even melted down some of the gold vessels used in church services in order to ransom prisoners. His priests followed Augustine's example of once a year calling the poor people of each parish together and giving them clothing. "Why am I a bishop? Why am I in the world?" Augustine asked. "Only to live as Jesus did," was his answer.

ST. AUGUSTINE

For thirty-five years Bishop Augustine was pastor to the people of Hippo. He usually preached twice each day, once at Mass in the morning and again at a service called Vespers in the evening. He was especially concerned that he correct the false information about the teachings of Jesus that heretics were spreading. He wrote several books, the most famous of which is his *Confessions,* which tells how he came to love Jesus and the Christian way of life. "You have made us, O God, for yourself, and our hearts shall find no rest until they rest with you," he wrote.

At age seventy-six, an extremely long life in the fifth century, Augustine still served the Church in North Africa, which was then slowly being overrun by the Vandals who swept down from northern Europe. During the siege of Hippo in 430, Bishop Augustine quietly died of a fever, praising God.

St. Augustine was first buried in St. Stephen's Church in Hippo, but years later his remains were reburied in Sardinia and then in Pavia, Italy. Most of his relics now lie in a splendid tomb in the cathedral of that city. In 1837, however, some of the saint's bones were returned to his homeland and placed in a church built on the ruins of Hippo.

Great teacher, preacher, and pastor that he was, St. Augustine is honored as a Doctor of the Church and is sometimes called the Doctor of Grace. He is also remembered as a patron of printers. Today, as for centuries, communities of sisters, brothers, and priests called Augustinians model their lives on some of St. Augustine's writings that form the *Rule of St. Augustine.*

St. Boniface

St. Boniface lived during the "Dark Ages," a time when the continent of Europe was in considerable distress. The once mighty Roman Empire had collapsed. Tribes of warriors from the north called Vandals were plundering the villages and ravaging the countryside. There was little stable government. Kings, queens, dukes, and princes were almost powerless. The people stayed close to their homes. The farmers scarcely plowed the fields. The storekeepers were afraid to open their shops. Schools were almost unheard of.

Boniface, though he is called the Apostle of Germany, grew up in England, the son of a nobleman. His family called him Winifrid. He did well in his classes, especially in history, writing, literature, and Bible study. When he was a teenager, he joined a Benedictine monastery. There he lived with the monks and each day worked and prayed according to a schedule established by St. Benedict almost two hundred years earlier. Winifrid decided to become a priest. He wanted to spend his life preaching the gospel to the Vandals who had settled along the Rhine River in Germany.

St. Boniface

b. about 680

d. June 5, 754

Apostle of Germany

Feast Day — June 5

Meaning of name — lucky, fortunate, from the Latin *bonifatus*

Latin
Bonifacius

Spanish, Protuguese
Bonifacio

Italian
Bonifacio
Bonifazio

German
Bonifaz
Bonifazius

English
Boniface
Bonny
Bonnie f.

Before the young priest Winifrid set out for Germany to meet the Vandals, he journeyed to Rome to receive the blessing of Pope Gregory II. The Pope encouraged Winifrid, since he knew that Germany needed many missionaries. For six years Winifrid preached the Good News and baptized many people in that hilly countryside along the Rhine.

Making converts to the Church was not easy work. The German people at that time believed in many gods, the chief of which was Thor, the god of thunder. His name is now given to Thursday, the fifth day of the week. As pagans these people worshiped a huge oak

112

SAINT BONIFACE

tree, which they considered sacred. They believed that if anyone touched that tree, Thor would immediately punish that person most severely.

Winifrid, however, knew that this was not true and set out to convince the people that such a belief was nonsense. One sunny morning Winifrid took a sharp axe, walked up to the tree, and with steady, deliberate strokes slowly chopped down the sacred oak. It crashed to the ground and broke into four huge pieces. The crowd, which had quickly gathered around Winifrid, was dumbfounded that no thunderbolts came down from Thor's heaven to kill Winifrid. They then knew that Winifrid's God was the true God. The wood of the once sacred oak was then used to build a Christian church.

Winifrid taught the German people that, while all the trees in the forest reflect God's majesty, the evergreen does so in a particular way. Summer or winter, fall or spring, its branches point heavenward to God. Ever green, they symbolize God's continuous presence in the world. For this reason Winifrid is responsible for the use of the Christmas tree, the *Tannenbaum*, as a symbol of God's Son being born as the Savior of the world.

Pope Gregory was pleased with Winifrid's missionary work and appointed him a bishop, calling him from then on by the name Boniface. Bishop Boniface continued his missionary duties, not only in Germany but also in France. He established schools and seminaries, built churches and monasteries. In many towns he discovered that some priests, and even bishops, were poorly trained for their work. To help them Bishop Boniface, as a special envoy of the Pope, presided at four meetings or synods of bishops. There he taught the bishops the latest teachings and rulings of the Church on how Christians should live and worship. Pope Gregory III made him an archbishop, and Pope Zachary named him the primate or the chief bishop of all Germany.

Despite high office and advancing age, Archbishop Boniface could not forget his years as a missionary. He resigned his position as the archbishop of Mainz and with fifty-two companions traveled north to Holland to preach the gospel. One day, as he was preparing to confirm some new Christians, a party of Vandals surprised the bishop and murdered him and his co-workers for the Lord. Boniface died a martyr in a mission land.

6. Founders of Religious Orders

St. Antony the Abbot

In Egypt over seventeen hundred years ago lived a young man named Antony. One morning at church he heard the priest read the gospel about what the young rich man should do to enter the gates of heaven. In this gospel Jesus told him to "sell all you have and give the money to the poor. . . . then come and follow me" (Luke 18:22). Then the gospel says that the young man "became very sad, because he was very rich."

Antony had many possessions, but the gospel that morning did not make him sorrowful. Rather, it made him wonder how he should spend his life. His father and mother had recently died, leaving him the heir to a considerable fortune of money and property. Antony could afford just about anything money could buy, but he decided to live a lifestyle where money was not very important. He decided to become a hermit, spending his days in prayer, self-denial, and almost complete solitude.

Antony was then about twenty years old. He gave his expensive clothes, his horses, the furniture of his house, and even the house itself to the poor. He saved just enough money to take care of his little sister, whom he sent to live with some holy women. For himself, Antony kept just a few simple clothes. The rich man's son was now a poor man.

For a while Antony still lived in his hometown of Coma in northern Egypt, but Coma was too busy and too noisy for a hermit. From an old man in the next village he learned how to live alone and be happy, how to pray, how to be satisfied with just the bare essentials. For several years Antony lived at some distance from Coma in an old cemetery. Some empty tombs provided him shelter from the rain and a place to sleep.

When Antony was about thirty-five, he moved his hermitage to an

---

St. Antony the Abbot

b. 251

d. 326

Father of All Monks

Feast Day — January 17

Meaning of name — after an esteemed Roman family called *Antonius*

French
Antoine
Antonie
Antoinette
Antonine   > f.
Toinette
Toinon

Spanish, Italian Portuguese
Antonio
Antonina f.

German
Anton
Antonius
Toni   m., f.
Antonie   f.

Norwegian
Antonia

English
Antony
Anthony
Tony
Antonia
Antoinette
Antonie
Net   > f.
Netty
Tonia
Tonya

abandoned fort in the desert, miles away from any neighbors. It wasn't long, however, before people came to Antony. They heard about his goodness and holiness. They wanted to talk to him, to ask his help in solving their problems, to pray with him. They wanted Antony to tell them how to find happiness. Antony had more visitors than many a non-hermit.

Sometimes for six months or longer Antony would remain in his hermitage, not seeing anyone, not even leaving for a walk. Visitors saw to it that he had enough to eat. They would climb onto the roof of his hermitage and lower loaves of bread to him by a rope, not talking to him, not disturbing his peace. Antony often ate only bread and drank only water. Instead of crunchy peanut butter, strawberry jam, or golden honey for his bread, he was satisfied with salt. Just one meal a day eaten at sunset—sometimes only one meal in two, three, or four days—was enough for Antony.

After about twenty years of desert living, Antony agreed to teach his many visitors how to live as a hermit. He realized that God wanted him to help others find the peace that he experienced. Antony was "greatly esteemed," which is what his name means. Soon other hermits set up one-person huts in the desert. On a regular basis Antony would talk with each hermit, telling them how to pray, how to think about God, how to free the body from distractions.

Because Antony was the first person to gather a group of hermits into a community, he is known today as the patriarch or Father of All Monks. Antony's monks did not follow a written rule, but they were united by a common spirit of prayer and love of God. Most of the time they lived alone in their one-room huts, apart from the others and from Antony, their abbot. Occasionally they would visit one another, pray together, and share their experiences.

Eventually Antony moved once more, this time at some distance to Mount Kolzim near the Red Sea. Occasionally for a good reason Antony would leave his mountain hermitage to help people. Once Athanasius, the bishop of Alexandria for forty years, asked Antony to preach against a heresy called Arianism. Antony was glad to do so. The Arian leaders were telling the people that Jesus was not the Son of God. Antony knew that the Arians couldn't be more wrong on that subject. He was then ninety years old, but he still could preach with enthusiasm to huge crowds.

Public officials respected Antony's wisdom and holiness. Often they went out of their way to meet him. The Roman emperor Constantine the Great asked Antony to pray for him. Once, when Antony refused to travel the long miles to Alexandria, a magistrate ordered his soldiers to march a group of prisoners to Mount Kolzim. When Antony heard about how much the prisoners, who at their best were sickly and weak, had suffered on that march, he agreed to talk to the commanding general. He answered the officer's questions, but he reminded him that a monk should value his solitude. Antony said, "As fish die if they are taken from the water, so does a monk wither away if he forsakes his solitude."

Antony was not afraid to put his life in danger to help others. At that time the Emperor Maximinian was cruelly persecuting the Christians in Egypt. Antony left Mount Kolzim and brought the suffering Christians food and clothing, prayed with them, consoled them. God spared Antony from Maximinian's cruelty.

Later, when a general named Balacius wanted to kill him, Antony in a letter told the general to "cease persecuting Christians, lest the wrath lay hold of you, for it is at hand." But that letter only made Balacius more determined to murder Antony. He set out for Antony's hermitage, but on that journey the horse of his companion Nestorius pulled Balacius off his own horse, biting him badly in the thigh. Balacius died three days later.

God gave Antony the power to cure sickness. Sometimes people waited near his hermitage for days, praying for a cure, and often they were cured. Antony reminded those who thanked him for the return of good health that it was God who should be thanked.

God also gave Antony the gift to immediately know about events which happened miles away from him. Once two monks started to cross the desert to visit Antony, but they became so thirsty that one of them died. At Mount Kolzim, more than a day's journey away, Antony realized what had happened. He at once orderd two other monks to hurry to them with some canteens of water. Antony said, "Run on the road towards Egypt; for of two who are coming one has just died and the other will do so if you do not hurry. For this has been shown to me as I prayed."

Antony lived to be age 105, proof indeed that a simple lifestyle is healthy. Antony was hardly ever sick and could see, hear, and think clearly to the day he died. When he realized that death was near, he went off with two of his monks to a secluded spot. He asked them to bury his body in an unmarked grave and not to tell anyone about it. Then Antony died at peace with God and with the world in the year 356.

That next year his friend Bishop Athanasius, now also a saint, wrote a rule for Antony's monks. Today monks in various parts of the world still follow this guide to living a holy life. Great scholars, such as St. Jerome and St. Augustine, have praised it for its sound advice.

Though St. Antony was blessed with good health through his long life, he is the patron of hospitalers, those who care for the sick. In the seventeenth century the Hospital Brothers of St. Antony were founded to care for the sick.

Artists picture Antony with a pig which has a bell attached to its neck. Sometimes Antony holds the bell. Two stories suggest how this image came about. Centuries ago people were forbidden in some cities to let their pigs run loose. Pigs dashing up and down the streets would scare horses and people and cause accidents. But the officials made an exception for hospitalers who owned pigs, as long as the pigs wore bells on their necks. The other story points to the pig as representing St. Antony's appetite, which he knew how to control carefully. Indeed, Antony did not eat pork chops or roasts, ham, or even an occasional slice of bacon. Also, the bell is a common symbol of hermits.

St. Antony is also remembered as the protector of farm animals, particularly pigs. Again, he is the patron of butchers, basketmakers, brushmakers, gravediggers, and graveyards. He is also a protector against epilepsy, as well as diseases of the skin, especially erysipelas. This disease is sometimes called the Sacred Fire or St. Antony's Fire. A person who suffers from erysipelas has a red skin rash and a high fever (pork fat was used to treat this disease).

Though St. Antony told those two monks to tell no one about his grave, it seems that they could not keep the secret. It is said that the saint's body was brought to Alexandria, then to Constantinople, and finally to a village near Vienne, France.

Sometimes St. Antony the Abbot is called St. Antony of Egypt or St. Antony the Great.

St. Benedict

In Italy fifteen hundred years ago a holy monk named Benedict set up a pattern of community living that is still practiced today. Benedict taught his followers, called Benedictines, how to worship and work. In a short book named the *Holy Rule,* Benedict left his monks and the world instructions on how such a life should be lived. Today priests, brothers, sisters, and lay people as well live according to Benedict's now famous *Rule.*

Benedict was born in Nursia, Italy, about the year 480. His well-to-do parents sent him to school in Rome, the capital city. But at age seventeen Benedict longed for a more peaceful and prayerful life than he found in Rome. Benedict first moved thirty-five miles away to Enfide, where he lived with some holy men. After a time Benedict decided to live alone as a hermit. His friend Romanus helped him build a simple hermitage in a cave at a place called Subiaco. Romanus gave him clothes made from sheepskin and regularly brought him food. For three years Benedict spent a quiet, prayerful life at Subiaco, but it was not as solitary as he had wanted it to be. Perhaps it was this cave-living experience which has led to St. Benedict being remembered as the patron of speleologists, that is, people who explore caves.

Benedict discovered that others would not let him live completely alone. They wanted to follow his way of knowing God and finding happiness. Even sons of wealthy Roman families joined him. Before long Benedict established a plan whereby twelve men would live together, one of them being the leader. These men came to be called monks (the Greek word *monachos* comes from *monos,* meaning

---

St. Benedict

b. about 480

d. about 547

Founder of Benedictine monasticism
Father of Western Monasticism

Feast Day — July 11

Meaning of name — blessed, from the Latin *benedictus*

French	*English*
Benoît	**Benedict**
Bénédicte	**Benedick**
Benoîte f.	**Banet**
	Benet
Spanish	**Bennet**
Benito	**Benson**
Benedicto	**Ben**
Benita f.	**Benny**
	Dix
Italian	**Dixon**
Benito	**Dixie**
Benedetto	**Benetta**
Benedetta f.	**Benita** f.
	Benicia
Portuguese	**Betta**
Benedicto	**Binnie**
Bento	
Benedicta f.	
Norwegian, Latin	
Benedictus	

"alone"). Benedict's monks worked, prayed, and shared meals together, but each day they had time to think and to pray by themselves.

Any group of people living together could not help but have some hard feelings or friction now and then. Benedict was gifted with the patience and wisdom to help his monks solve their problems. Once, however, some monks who thought Benedict was too strict tried to kill him with a glass of poisoned wine. But when Benedict prayed a blessing over the wine before drinking it, the glass shattered. Perhaps that is why St. Benedict is the patron of those who have been poisoned.

When an evil priest near Subiaco continued to make life difficult for his monks, Benedict decided to build a monastery atop a mountain near the town of Cassino, which is on the highway to Naples in southern Italy. Benedict's monastery of Monte Cassino flourishes to this day. It has been totally rebuilt twice, first after 577 when barbarians destroyed it, and again after 1943 and its devastation during World War II.

At Monte Cassino the monks lived in one large house, rather than in groups of twelve. Benedict was called the abbot or father of the monks. Soon the monastery added guest rooms for visitors. Farmers, businessmen, students, craftsmen, Church dignitaries, and even a cruel king, Totila the Goth, traveled many miles to Monte Cassino. They wanted to see firsthand how the Benedictines lived. King Totila left the monastery a changed man. From that day forward he governed the Goths sensibly and made peace with his enemies.

Though the Benedictines lived quietly apart from the world in their hilltop monastery, each day they cared for the sick and the poor for miles around Cassino. Anyone who stopped at the monastery looking for a place to stay, for some food, or for some advice, was never turned away. Once during a local famine Benedict gave away all the food in the abbey's kitchen, except for five loaves of bread. Benedict knew that God would provide for his monks. He was right. The next day someone left two hundred bushels of flour at the monastery's gate. That was enough flour to bake dozens of loaves of bread for weeks to come.

Benedict's *Holy Rule,* which he wrote at Monte Cassino, has but a brief introduction and seventy-three tiny chapters. They are packed with sound advice on how to live at peace and how to seek God. The *Rule* has been so widely followed that St. Benedict is called the Father of Western Monasticism. The *Rule* tells how to set up and govern a monastery, how to pray, eat, work, dress, and even sleep. "Do not sleep with knives at your sides." "Treat every visitor as if he were Christ." "Keep a candle burning at night."

Benedict organized the day into times of prayer, reading, and work. "Worship and work" became the Benedictine motto. In whatever the monks did during the day and in whomever they met, they were to seek God. God could be found in the person of the abbot, in each monk, and in each visitor. That is why guests have always been welcome at Benedictine monasteries and convents.

Scholastica, Benedict's sister, with her brother's help, established the Benedictine way of life for women who joined her convent (see next story on p. 124).

In time Benedict established the Monastery of St. Stephen at Terracina, but Monte Cassino remained his headquarters. It was there that he died in the year 547. Six days before he died he told his monks to dig his grave. Shortly after it was dug, he became sick with a fever. He died while standing at prayer in the chapel one morning after receiving Holy Communion. His monks buried him next to his sister at Monte Cassino.

There's a story that in the eighth century the bones of Benedict and Scholastica were moved to the French abbey at Fleury-sur-Loire. But another account tells that at the order of Pope Zachary relics of the saints' bodies were returned to Monte Cassino.

St. Benedict's teachings continue to provide the twentieth-century world with wisdom and guidance. At monasteries such as Monte Cassino, Italy; Montserrat, Spain; Solesmes, France; Downside, England; Fulda, Germany; Melk, Austria; and Collegeville, Minnesota, the *Holy Rule* is followed. Even lay people who live directly in the hubbub of the world—handling their jobs and professions, raising families, and praising God however they might—often follow the *Rule* as far as possible. They are called Oblates. Benedict left sound advice for all people: "Everyone has his own gift from God, one in this way and another in that."

In 1964 Pope Paul VI named St. Benedict the patron of Europe. He is also remembered as the patron of those who suffer from fevers, kidney trouble, and inflammatory diseases such as rheumatoid arthritis.

SAINT
SCHOLASTICA

St. Scholastica

Now and then a family tree lists more than one saint among the relatives. To name a few: the brothers Cosmas and Damian, Cyril and Methodius, Andrew and Peter, James and Jude; the sisters Rufina and Secunda and Victoria and Anatolia; there are Augustine and his mother Monica. Also, among others, there are Benedict and Scholastica, a brother and a sister, who are saints.

Scholastica admired how Benedict and his monks followed a peaceful daily schedule of work and prayer at their monastery of Monte Cassino in southern Italy. Scholastica wanted to live as the monks did, following the *Holy Rule* which Benedict wrote to guide his followers.

> **St. Scholastica**
>
> *b.* about 480
>
> *d.* about 547
>
> **Founder of the Benedictine sisters**
>
> **Feast Day — February 10**
>
> **Meaning of name — to have leisure, from the Greek *scholastikos***
>
> | *Latin* | *English* |
> |---|---|
> | **Scholasticus** | **Scholastica** |

Years earlier, as a small child, Scholastica told God that she would be of service to him. Now, following the advice of Benedict, Scholastica established a convent or home for women who lived, prayed, and worked together. This convent of the first Benedictine sisters was near the foot of Monte Cassino at a place called Plombariola. Benedict's monks lived at the top of that mountain in their monastery. It was a rewarding life of worship and work at both the monastery and the convent.

Though they lived almost on the same block, Benedict and Scholastica preferred their life of prayer and solitude so much that they visited only once a year. Pope St. Gregory the Great in his life of St. Benedict tells us about the last visit that this brother and sister had together. It was the year 547 or close to it. As was their custom, Benedict met Scholastica at a picnic shelter about halfway down the mountainside. A few of Benedict's monks joined them for the visit.

Benedict and Scholastica spent the day "enjoying the mutual comfort of heavenly talk," writes St. Gregory. Toward evening Scholastica suggested to Benedict that they continue their visit through the night. They were getting on in years and Scholastica feared that she might never see her brother again. But Benedict, surprised at the question, told his sister, "You know I can't stay longer. You know that I must obey the *Rule* just like anyone else." The *Rule* did not permit monks to stay outside the monastery overnight.

That evening the sky was clear and blue, not a cloud in sight. Scholastica bowed her head and prayed that God would somehow answer her wish. Almost instantly the weather changed; it began to thunder and lightning as never before. Soon rain fell in a downpour. It rained so hard that Benedict and his monks would be drenched if they stepped outside the door. In that storm it would have been foolish to start hiking up the mountain to the monastery.

"God forgive you, sister!" Benedict said, "What have you done?"

Scholastica answered, "I asked you to stay a little longer and you would not listen. So I asked God and he listened."

Thus, through the night Benedict, Scholastica, and the others chatted and listened to the rain patter on the roof of the picnic shelter. The next morning after breakfast Benedict and his monks said good-bye to Scholastica and hiked back up the mountain to their monastery. That was the last time that Benedict and Scholastica saw each other.

Three days later when Benedict was standing in his room at Monte Cassino he had a vision of Scholastica's soul flying up to heaven as a white dove. Benedict told his brother monks about his dear sister's death and sent them to Plombariola to bring her body back to the monastery for her funeral. Benedict decided to bury Scholastica in the grave which his monks had prepared for him. It was not long before Benedict joined Scholastica. In just three weeks he too died, and his monks buried him next to his sister in the same grave.

St. Scholastica is the patron of the thousands of Benedictine sisters across the world. February 10, her feast day, is a special day for all the daughters of Scholastica. Benedictine sisters in convents, schools, hospitals, parishes, and elsewhere serve God and his people by their worship and work. To this day people pray to St. Scholastica for protection against storms. She is remembered also as the patron of children who suffer from seizures.

St. Dominic

The Church in the twelfth century faced a difficult challenge. Perhaps more than ever before, people called heretics were teaching false information about Jesus and the kingdom of God. Unfortunately, many of the priests were not well educated and could not adequately correct the heretics, especially a group called the Albigensians.

In Spain there lived a young priest named Dominic, a priest well trained in the truths which Jesus taught. His bishop, Diego d'Azevedo, asked Dominic, who was a brilliant preacher, to join him in the Church's campaign against the heretics.

For ten years Dominic preached the Good News of Jesus throughout southern France. It did not take long for the heretics to fear his powerful and convincing sermons. Whenever Dominic was scheduled to preach, a crowd gathered and listened intently to him. The Albigensian preachers had no chance at all. Dominic's knowledge of the Bible and religion, along with his skills as a speaker, made the heretics' efforts look ridiculous. In fact, many a listener to Dominic's sermons went home from church that day convinced that they should work closely with him and be his followers.

It was not long before white-robed priests and brothers called Dominicans staffed many parishes and schools across Europe. By the year 1216 Dominic's "Order of Preachers" was firmly established. Dominic insisted that his preachers be well educated. Whenever a house—a "friary," as the Dominicans called it—was set up in a new community, Dominic sent a professor to live there. That Dominican

St. Dominic

b. 1170
d. August 6, 1221

Founder of the Order of Preachers (Dominicans)

Feast Day — August 8

Meaning of name — belonging to the Lord, from the Latin *Dominicus*

French
Dominique

Spanish
Domingo

Italian
Domenico
Domenica f.

German
Dominik
Dominikus
Monika f.

English
Dominic
Dominick
Dom
Dommy
Demmy
Monica
Myrna } f.
Morna

SAINT DOMINIC

would teach the young friars how to preach the Word of God. Dominic also asked women to form convents and live the Dominican way of life as sisters. He even called upon lay people to join his Order as *tertiaries* or members of the "Third Order."

Before Dominic's death in 1221, his Dominicans were preaching the gospel not only in Spain, Italy, and France but also in Hungary, Morocco, Denmark, the Holy Land, Poland, and elsewhere. As priests, brothers, sisters, and lay tertiaries, the Dominicans followed the motto: "To contemplate and to give others the fruits of contemplation." A Dominican was committed to study and to learn the Word of God and then to share that knowledge with others.

Once Dominic and Francis of Assisi met in Rome. Neither of them fully realized how the Orders they founded made it possible for the Church to reach the hearts and souls of multitudes of people, both in the cities and in the rural areas. Both Dominic and Francis insisted that their followers live simply as did Jesus, having the bare essentials. They did not travel on horseback or in carriages; they walked. They did not stay in fancy hotels or dine at expensive restaurants; they stayed at their friaries or at reasonable accommodations.

There is a tradition that St. Dominic himself *established* the prayer devotion called the Rosary, but this is not true. Both the practice of praying 50 or 150 Hail Marys and the use of beads to count prayers were common long before St. Dominic's time. What is true on this subject, however, is that since the late fifteenth century, more than two centuries after their founder died, the Dominicans have fostered this devotion. To this day in praying the Rosary, Christians think about the birth, crucifixion, and resurrection of Jesus while reciting over and over the Our Father, Hail Mary, and Glory Be—the prayers which form the Rosary.

Frequently artists picture St. Dominic beside a small black and white dog that has a torch in its mouth. The Dominicans have been called the watchdogs of the Lord, which in Latin is *Domini canes*. The torch in the dog's mouth symbolizes the "light of the world" or the truths of the kingdom of God which the Dominicans preach and teach wherever they work throughout the world.

In the year 1234 Pope Gregory IX canonized St. Dominic. His body is buried in the Church of Santo Domenico in Bologna, Italy. St. Dominic truly "belongs to the Lord," which is the meaning of his name.

St. Francis of Assisi

Today, as for over seven hundred years, brown or black-robed priests, brothers, and sisters staff thousands of parishes, hospitals, shrines, schools, and homes for the poor. There they continue the work of their founder, St. Francis of Assisi, who worked daily with the poor.

Francis Bernardone, the son of a wealthy cloth merchant, grew up in Assisi, a city in the mountain country of northern Italy. As a young man Francis squandered his father's money on fancy clothes, parties, and good times. In fact, Francis entertained his friends so frequently and so lavishly that they called him "the

St. Francis of Assisi

b. 1181 or 1182

d. October 3, 1226

Founder of the Franciscans

Feast Day — October 4

For other name forms of Francis, *see* story about St. Frances Xavier Cabrini on p. 24.

king of the feasts." But something deep in his heart told Francis that such expensive living was unnecessary, especially when many poor families in Assisi and elsewhere had scarcely enough to eat. At about age twenty-five Francis made up his mind to change his lifestyle dramatically. From then on Francis lived with as few possessions as possible and spent his time vigorously teaching the poor about the gospel of Jesus. To this day Francis is known as *Il Poverello* or "The Poor One."

Francis dressed in a coarse brown robe, tied with a rope for a belt. That was how the Italian peasants who worked the fields dressed. He said that Lady Poverty was his wife. It was not long before other people in Assisi, following Francis' example, decided to give their belongings to the poor and to join Francis. First he had three followers— Bernard, Peter, and Giles—but soon there were eleven. At that point Francis decided to write down a rule to guide their lives. Francis in his rule emphasized the gospel message to care for one another with love.

Francis called his followers "Friars Minor" because they lived as the poor or minor people of Italy did in the early thirteenth century. Today we know the members of this religious Order by the term *Franciscans.* Thousands of Francis' followers sign the initials of the Order, O.F.M., after their names.

The friars usually walked two-by-two about Assisi, the nearby towns, and the countryside. They talked to the farmers working the fields, gave homilies on the church steps or in the shopping centers. By their example and good works the Franciscans showed that all

O lord our christ,
     may i have your mind
     and your spirit.
make me an instrument
     of your peace.
where there is hatred,
     let me sow love,
where there is injury,
     pardon,
where there is discord,
     union,
where there is doubt,
     faith,
where there is despair,
     hope,
where there is darkness,
     light,
where there is sadness,
     joy,
for your mercy
     and for your truth's
     sake.

St. Francis of Assisi

men and women are brothers and sisters who should help one another. The friars begged each day for food and a little money to buy what they needed and to care for the poor—people who were hungry or needed a home, comfort, and friends.

Francis and his friars saw God's glory in all his creatures—people, birds, animals, flowers, plants, and even the rocks which formed the hills and valleys near Assisi. To this day, often a statue of this saint is placed in a park or a garden to remind us of Francis' love of God's creatures. In fact, in 1979 Pope John Paul II proclaimed St. Francis the patron of ecology. The Pope said that Francis "considered nature a wonderful gift of God to humanity, to the point that, inspired by a practical divine spirit, he sang that most beautiful 'Canticle of the Sun' through which he gave praise, glory, honor, and every blessing to the most high, the almighty good Lord." This prayer begins: "Praise to thee, my Lord, for all thy creatures, above all Brother Sun who brings us the day and lends us his light."

Within ten years the Franciscans were well known up and down Italy, as well as in France, Spain, and Germany. In another ten years the Order numbered over five thousand members. They gathered in 1221 for an important meeting at the friary of Portiuncula, which was Francis' headquarters in Assisi.

By this time, too, a woman named Clare, with Francis' help, established the first convent of Franciscan nuns in Assisi. Today these sisters are called Poor Clares, one of the many groups of Franciscan nuns. The Poor Clares live very simply in seclusion, each day spending hours in prayer.

As the numbers in his Order increased, Francis traveled hundreds of miles to direct the work and lives of his brothers. Once he walked to Rome to receive the blessing of Pope Innocent III on the work of the Friars

Minor. Francis also visited the Holy Land. To this day, Franciscan friars care for the Holy Places where important events in the life of Jesus occurred. Following Jesus has always been the most important goal in life for the Franciscans.

While in Rome in 1223, Francis told Pope Honorius III about his plans to build a crib scene to celebrate the birth of the Christ Child. Leaving Rome, Francis arrived at Greccio near Assisi on Christmas Eve that year. There with the help of his friend Giovanni Velita he constructed a crib in the church and arranged figures of the Blessed Virgin and St. Joseph, a donkey, an ox, and the shepherds who came to adore the newborn Savior. At midnight Mass that evening Francis, a deacon, sang the gospel account that describes Jesus' birth at Bethlehem. That Christmas season custom of building a crib scene in homes, parishes, schools, and public places continues to this day.

Before Francis died at age forty-five, a young man by today's standards, the wounds which Jesus suffered during his passion and crucifixion appeared on Francis' body. In that special way Jesus, the Son of God, permitted Francis to share in his suffering which redeemed the world. About two years after his death, Pope Gregory IX proclaimed Francis a saint.

In 1981 and 1982 the world took special note of St. Francis of Assisi as it marked the eight hundredth anniversary of his birth. Among the ceremonies was the release by the United States Postal Service on October 7, 1982, of a $.20 commemorative stamp bearing an image of Francis and a flock of doves, the birds of peace. The first-day ceremonies for the stamp took place in San Francisco, California, the best known of the many American communities named after this saint of peace.

St. Francis of Assisi is the patron of Italy and merchants.

St. Ignatius of Loyola

From Japan to Canada, from Brazil to Portugal, from one end of the world to the other live priests and brothers called Jesuits. After their names they write "S.J.," which stands for the "Society of Jesus." That is the official name of a Congregation of thousands of men who follow the motto: "To the greater glory of God." Jesuits work in hospitals and orphanages, in retirement centers and parishes—wherever people gather to listen to the message of Jesus. It was Ignatius of Loyola who began the Society of Jesus over four hundred years ago.

Ignatius was the youngest of eight sons among the eleven children of the governor of Oñaz and Loyola in northern Spain. His parents named their last son Inigo after a Spanish Benedictine saint. But after Ignatius established the Jesuits, he called himself Ignatius in honor of an earlier saint by that name, Ignatius of Antioch.

As a young man Ignatius did not dream of starting a religious Congregation. He was more than satisfied with his position as a servant to the treasurer of the Spanish government. Later he worked in the house of an important officer in King Ferdinand's navy. That experience led Ignatius to become a soldier in the king's army, a career he loved. While a soldier's life was dangerous and uncertain, it was also exciting and challenging.

In 1521, when Ignatius was thirty, his lifestyle changed dramatically. During a battle at Pampeluna, Spain, Ignatius was seriously wounded. A cannon ball ripped through his legs, leaving his right shin broken and his left calf torn open. Ignatius went home to the Loyola Castle, where he had been born, to recuperate. There the doctors found that his leg had been poorly set on the battlefield and that it needed to be rebroken and reset. And after that painful experience,

---

St. Ignatius of Loyola

b. 1491

d. July 31, 1556

Founder of the Society of Jesus (Jesuits)

Feast Day — July 31

Meaning of name — fiery, from the Greek *ignatios*

Latin, Norwegian	*English*
Ignatius	Ignatius
French	Ignacia f.
Ignace	Iggy
Spanish, Portuguese	Nash
Ignacio	
Italian	
Ignazio	
Ignacio	
German	
Ignaz	
Polish	
Ignacy	

St. Ignatius of Loyola

the end of the bone stuck out under his knee. Then, in another operation, the doctors cut the bone away. Ignatius was a strong man. He endured pain patiently, even though there was no sedation as there is today. Though Ignatius recovered nicely, from then on he walked with a limp.

While lying in bed week after week, Ignatius asked his family for some books to read to pass the time. The only books available were one about the life of Jesus and another about the lives of the saints. Ignatius had read many books in his day, but none such as these. He decided that he could be like St. Francis and St. Benedict. He wanted to dedicate his life to God and command an army of followers who would preach the Good News to anyone who would listen.

As soon as Ignatius recovered, he hurried to the Benedictine abbey of Montserrat in northeast Spain. There he prayed for many hours to the Blessed Virgin, to whom he had a special devotion. While at prayer he made up his mind to give up his promising career as a soldier. He left his sword on Mary's altar in the chapel, gave his armor to a beggar, and went off to the nearby town of Manresa. There Ignatius cared for the sick in a hospital as a first step in planning a life of service to God. During the next year he started to write his now famous *Spiritual Exercises,* a series of instructions on how to pray. Today, as for four centuries, Jesuits and non-Jesuits alike frequently study these meditations as a help to prayer.

A year later, in 1523, Ignatius briefly visited the Holy Land where Jesus lived. Since war and turmoil ravaged that land, Ignatius came home to Spain and decided to return to school. He wanted to study theology and philosophy to learn as much as he could about the presence of God in the world. But since Ignatius had not been to school in years, he first had to review the basic subjects in a grade-school classroom. There Ignatius, a man of thirty-three, sat with children patiently studying his lessons. Eleven years later, after attending classes at Spanish and French universities, Ignatius earned a master's degree.

At this point in his life, Ignatius realized that he was ready to start a religious Congregation. The date was August 15, 1534, the feast of the Assumption of the Blessed Mother. Ignatius and six companions, one of them a priest, another Francis Xavier, now a saint, gathered at St. Denis Chapel at Montmartre. At this famous church in Paris, France, the seven men promised to serve God as a group. They hoped to work in the Holy Land, but if that were not possible, wherever the Pope would send them. A year later three more companions joined the Jesuits, but war prevented the ten from traveling to the Holy Land. They decided to ask Pope Paul III to bless them and to assign them work.

When Pope Paul read the constitutions or the rules which Ignatius had written for the Jesuits, he said, "The finger of God is here." In 1537 he gave Ignatius and his Jesuits special permission to be ordained priests. Three years later Pope Paul officially approved the Society of Jesus. Ignatius became the first general or leader of this little army of Jesuits.

The rules of the Society were, in part, unlike those of other religious Congregations. Ignatius wanted his followers to work daily close to the people. The Jesuits preached, heard confessions, gave spiritual advice, and taught school. They did not wear a special habit or uniform. They did not sing prayers in church several times a day as monks do. They prayed wherever they worked.

New members of the Society spent two years as novices, rather than one as was customary in other Congregations. These two years were devoted to prayer and training to understand the spirit of the Jesuit way of life. Besides making to God the traditional vows of poverty, chastity, and obedience, the Jesuits promised special obedience to the Pope.

The Holy Father sent the Jesuits to distant lands as missionaries, but Ignatius remained in Rome to supervise their work. He wrote more than six thousand letters of advice and encouragement to his men. He also finished writing his *Spiritual Exercises,* and he established two schools in Rome, as well as a house for penitent women and a house for Jews who had become Christians. Ignatius was frequently sick, but he nevertheless kept a busy work schedule. In 1551 he asked his Jesuits to elect someone else as their general, but they refused. His men did not want a new leader.

For five more years until his sudden death in July, 1556, Ignatius worked for the greater glory of God. At its founder's death the Society of Jesus numbered about a thousand members in 101 houses in twelve provinces or divisions throughout the world. In 1980, almost 450 years later, over 27,000 Jesuits served the Church.

St. Ignatius is buried in the Gesu Church—the Jesus Church—in Rome. In 1622 Pope Gregory XV named Ignatius a saint. Three hundred years later, in 1922, Pope Pius XI honored St. Ignatius of Loyola by declaring him the patron of spiritual exercises and retreats.

7. Doctors of the Church

St. Jerome

More than sixteen centuries ago, a boy named Eusebius Hieronymus Sophronius grew up in northeastern Italy. His country was then part of the mighty Roman Empire. The language taught in the schools and spoken by the educated people was Latin. That language, as well as Greek and Hebrew, Eusebius learned expertly in the classroom and by self-study. Years later he wrote important books in these languages, books which have contributed much knowledge to the world.

In English-speaking countries, Eusebius is known today as Jerome, the translation from Latin of his middle name. When Jerome was twelve years old, his parents sent him to Rome to the school of a famous teacher named Donatus. There for seven years Jerome studied languages, science, and other subjects. He also learned much about his religion.

Jerome's parents were Christians, but he had not been baptized as a baby, which was customary at the time. But, at age nineteen, on Easter Day in the year 366, Jerome was baptized by the Holy Father himself, Pope Liberius.

St. Jerome

b. about 342

d. September 30, 420

Doctor of the Church

Feast Day — September 30

Meaning of name — bearing a holy name, from the Greek *hierônymos*

Latin, German
Hieronymus

French
Jérôme

Spanish
Jerónimo
Jeromo

Italian
Geronimo
Girolamo

Portuguese
Jeronimo

Norwegian
Jerome

English
Gerome
Jerome
Jerry
Jere
Jer

Jerome decided that a change of scenery would do him good and thus set off on a trip. For a while he lived with a group of priests and laymen in a monastery. Eventually he visited Syria in the Near East. For two years in a desert called Chalcis, he lived the simple life of a hermit. He said that he had "no other company but scorpions and wild beasts." Those years gave Jerome time to think, pray, plan his life, and learn Hebrew, the language spoken in Palestine.

Jerome's friend Paulinus, the bishop of Antioch, realized that

ST. JEROME

Jerome was a learned and holy young man. When Jerome left the desert, Paulinus ordained him a priest. Gradually, the talents of this young priest became known even to the Pope. Thus in the year 382 Pope Damasus I called Jerome, Bishop Paulinus, and others to Rome for an important meeting. Jerome then stayed in Rome and became the Pope's secretary.

Pope Damasus asked Jerome to take on the important job of translating the New Testament into the modern Latin language. The New Testament is the part of the Bible which describes the life and teachings of Jesus and his Church. Jerome, therefore, reworked the twenty-seven books of the New Testament. Only a few very learned people such as Jerome understood the old Latin language. The result of Jerome's work was a translation which thousands and thousands of people who knew modern Latin could then read and understand.

Jerome did not stay long in Rome. He had enemies, especially some priests who did not like his preaching to them about living simple lives. Again Jerome traveled widely before making his home at Bethlehem in the Holy Land about the year 385. There in a monastery he continued to write and translate. He also opened a school for boys.

Again Jerome worked on a major project, translating the Old Testament, the first main division of the Bible, into modern Latin from Hebrew. The creation account, the lives of Abraham, Moses, Jeremiah, Ruth, Samson, David, Daniel, etc., and of God's caring for the Israelites, the Chosen People, could now be understood by great numbers of people who could read Latin but not Hebrew. Of the forty-six books of the Old Testament, Jerome translated all but five. This translation, along with his New Testament work, came to be known as the *Vulgate,* which means "common" in Latin. Today, some sixteen centuries later, scholars who prepare new translations of the Bible often study Jerome's *Vulgate* as a help to their work. It was a magnificent accomplishment. St. Jerome is sometimes called the Father of Biblical Science.

For almost thirty-five years Jerome lived in Bethlehem. His monastery provided food and shelter to thousands of refugees. These homeless people fled Rome and other cities in the Roman Empire, which was then largely ungoverned. Savages called Vandals were looting and burning their way across the empire, killing anyone who stood in their way.

In the year 416 Jerome's monastery was burned by these marauders. Four years later, Jerome, a tired old man, perhaps the most learned man of his age, died in Bethlehem. His body is buried in the Church of the Nativity, which was built on the spot where Jesus was born. Later Jerome's bones were reburied in Rome.

Because of his important work as a translator of the Bible and other books, St. Jerome has been honored as a Doctor of the Church. Artists have pictured this saint as an old man with books and a pen, sometimes wearing glasses. German artists have painted him in the scarlet robes of a cardinal and working in his office. This interpretation is not entirely accurate, however, since St. Jerome was not a cardinal, even though he was secretary to Pope Damasus. It was only much later in the history of the Church that the papal secretary has been a cardinal.

Other artists portray St. Jerome in his study, sitting next to a lion, which is a symbol of a cardinal. Also, there's a story told that Jerome once removed a thorn from a lion's paw. While such an account is obviously fiction, the artist had a point: a lion is a mighty beast of the jungle. Jerome is a mighty saint of the Church.

St. Jerome is the patron of librarians and students.

Pope St. Gregory the Great

If a person's name has "the Great" after it, that is something to brag about. It means that a particular man or woman used his or her talents and blessings to accomplish great things. Pope St. Gregory I was one of "the Greats." He once stopped a powerful general from destroying Rome. He wrote books which are still read thirteen centuries later. As the Pope he ruled the Church wisely for fourteen years. He was a *prefect* or mayor of Rome. He is called the Apostle of England. A type of Church music, Gregorian chant, is named after him. He is a Doctor of the Church. Pope St. Gregory I was a great man.

Being a saint ran in Gregory's family. His mother is St. Silvia and his two aunts are St. Tarsilla and St. Aemiliana. His father Gordianus was a Roman senator. Like his father, Gregory became a public official. At age thirty he was a mayor of the city. Rome then faced hard times. The Roman Empire, at one time the greatest world power, had collapsed. The emperor had fled the city for Constantinople, more than a thousand miles away. Lombards, barbarians from the North, were sweeping down upon Italy, pillaging and destroying whatever was in their path. It was a difficult time.

Pope St. Gregory the Great

b. 540
d. March 12, 604

Apostle of England

Doctor of the Church

Feast Day — September 3

Meaning of name — vigilant, from the Greek *grĕgorios*

Latin
Gregorius

French
Grégoire

Spanish, Italian
Gregorio

German
Gregorius
Gregor

Norwegian
Gregor

English
Gregory
Greg
Gregg

In the year 574 Gregory decided to become a monk, but the Romans would not for long let him give up public life. When his father died, Gregory turned his family's spacious house on Rome's Caelian Hill into a monastery named after St. Andrew. Six of his father's properties in Sicily also became monasteries.

For the next five years Gregory lived as a monk. Then in 579 the Pope asked Gregory to leave the quiet and peace of his monastery and take on a very important position. The Pope appointed Gregory as

141

the ambassador to the court of the emperor. There in Constantinople Gregory carefully tended to his duties, but he did not live the grand life of receptions, banquets, and ceremonies common to that career. He preferred to live quietly and prayerfully with the monks who came with him.

In 586 Gregory returned to Rome as an advisor to Pope Pelagius II and as the abbot of St. Andrew's Monastery. Three years later a plague ravaged the Eternal City. The Tiber River overflowed its banks, flooding blocks of buildings and ruining all the grain in the Church's granaries. The Romans were dying of disease as "though they were shot down by arrows from the sky," said Gregory. Among the dead was Pope Pelagius. Without hesitation the clergy and the citizens of Rome elected Gregory as their new Pope. The plague continued to claim many lives each day. Pope Gregory called upon the Romans to join him in pilgrimages to pray at holy places in the city. The response was fantastic. Crowds of people followed the Pope about the city in fervent prayer. God's answer to their prayers was soon apparent; the plague disappeared.

Like Popes John XXIII, Paul VI, and John Paul I and II in the 1960s, '70s, and '80s, Pope Gregory I in the 590s cared deeply about his flock. He was worried that many people were hungry and homeless and often without priests and teachers to look after their souls. Gregory was a humanitarian and a peacemaker. When a corn shortage came, he opened the Church's granaries at regular intervals to the poor. When the Lombards were about to attack Rome, the Romans looked to this Pope more than to the civil officials to protect them. In 593 Pope Gregory bravely left the safety of the walled city for a meeting with the Lombard general Agilulf. He convinced Agilulf, without shooting a single arrow, to accept taxes each year from the Romans. Thus Rome and much of Italy was spared destruction.

Pope Gregory was blessed with a missionary spirit. Years earlier he had set out with some monks to bring the Word of God to England. At that time England or Britannia was a fearsome place, almost at the end of the world. Gregory never made it to England, however, since the Pope called him back to Rome for other duties. Years later Pope Gregory happened to see two fair-haired and light-skinned English boys in Rome's main shopping center. These boys were an unusual sight in Rome, since the native Romans have a tanned skin. They are "angels, not Angles," said Gregory in a now famous remark. "Alleluias must be sung in Aella's land"—Aella was then a king in England. Gregory wanted the people who lived in that distant island nation to hear the Word of God. He sent St. Augustine of Canterbury to evangelize them. With forty other monks from St. Andrew's, Augustine preached the Good News of Jesus to the English. An English historian named Bede said about Pope Gregory: "If he be not an apostle to others, he is one to us."

In fourteen years Pope Gregory crowded in enough work as the chief bishop of the Church to exhaust a lifetime of energy. He established a boys' choir to sing at special Masses and ceremonies at the Vatican, the headquarters of the Church. For centuries that choir continued its splendid singing. Pope Gregory appointed *rectors* to administer some eighteen hundred square miles of property which the Church then held in Italy, Africa, and elsewhere. The papal household, where Pope Gregory lived simply as a monk, was also reorganized. He set the boundaries of dioceses and directed how bishops should govern them.

Pope Gregory was an excellent administrator. Three hundred years later King Alfred in England ordered that every new bishop be given a copy of Pope Gregory's book on the office of bishop and the care of souls. The Pope also encouraged musicians to develop a style of Church music that bears his name yet today—Gregorian chant. His friend Deacon Peter said that Pope Gregory never rested; indeed, he was a very busy man.

Artists often picture Pope Gregory sitting with a dove resting on his shoulder. The dove may be poking its beak into the Pope's mouth. It seems that the dove is talking to Gregory, who, in turn, is dictating sentences,

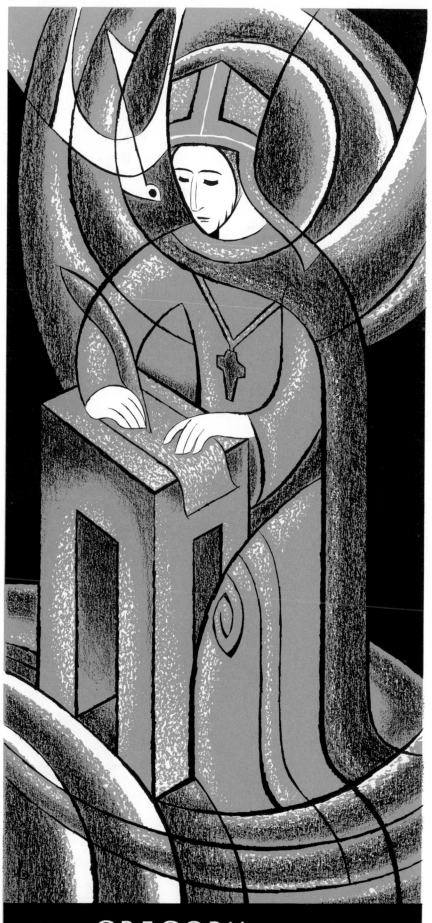

ST. GREGORY the GREAT

or perhaps music, to be written down by a secretary. Since the dove is a symbol of the Holy Spirit, this image tells us that God gave Pope Gregory many talents as a writer. Among his books is a collection of saints' stories. From Pope Gregory, more than from anyone else, we have learned about St. Benedict. Pope Gregory admired Benedict's prayerful and quiet lifestyle.

For one who lived in the seventh century and who suffered much sickness, especially stomach trouble, frequent fevers, and a condition called gout, Pope Gregory lived a long life. He died in the year 604 at age sixty-four. One of his last acts before his death was to send a warm winter coat to a poor bishop. Pope Gregory remembered always that he was a ''Servant of the Servants of God,'' as he called himself. That title is one of the Pope's titles to this day.

Pope Gregory was buried in St. Peter's Basilica at the Vatican. The epitaph on his tomb noted that he was ''God's *consul*'' (a *consul* was an important Roman official). His body, which was moved several times, now rests in the Clementine Chapel in the basilica. Great teacher that he was, he has been honored as a Doctor of the Church. He is the patron of teachers and scholars as well as musicians and singers.

St. Bernard of Clairvaux

In the year 1111 a young man of twenty-one named Bernard decided to join a very strict Order of monks called Cistercians at a new monastery named Cîteaux in France. This decision did not at first set too well with Bernard's noble parents. They did not mind him leaving their castle near Dijon in eastern France to become a monk, but they were horrified that he would join an almost unknown monastery and one where the daily routine was so strict.

But Bernard had made up his mind. In fact, the more he talked about it, the more his relatives and neighbors decided to join him at Cîteaux. He was like the Pied Piper of Hamelin, whose peppy music convinced all the children to follow him out of town. Thirty-one of Bernard's family and friends, including his brothers Gerard, Guy, Andrew, and Bartholomew, his uncle Gauldry, and his cousin Robert, joined that monastery with Bernard. Later his aged father Tesselin and his youngest brother Nicard, who had stayed home to care for Tesselin, also became monks.

St. Bernard of Clairvaux

b. 1090

d. August 20, 1153

Founder of the Cistercians
Doctor of the Church

Feast Day — August 20

Meaning of name — bold as a bear, from the German *bernhard*

Latin	
Bernardus	**Bernhardine f.**
French	*Norwegian*
Bernard	**Bernhard**
Bernardin	
Bernadette f.	*English*
	Bernard
Spanish	**Barnard**
Bernardo	**Bernie**
Bernal	**Barney**
	Berney
Italian	**Bernarr**
Bernardo	**Barnet**
Bernardino	**Ben**
German	**Bernardine ⌐f.**
Bernd	**Bernardina ⌐**
Bernhard	

Three years after Bernard came to Cîteaux, he was elected abbot of a new Cistercian monastery at Clairvaux, which means "valley of light." Twelve monks moved to this monastery with Abbot Bernard. There they lived most simply. Bernard said that "whatever goes beyond bare nourishment and simple plain clothing" was unnecessary. During those first years at Clairvaux, the monks scarcely had the necessities to keep body and soul together. On many days they ate little else than coarse barley bread and soup made from boiled beech tree leaves. With that diet it's not surprising that Bernard suffered from stomach trouble and migraine headaches much of the time.

Because Bernard did much to plan and to influence the way of life

St.
Bernard
of
Clairvaux

of the Cistercian monks, he is considered a founder of that Order. The Cistercians, like the Benedictines, follow the *Holy Rule* of St. Benedict. But the Cistercians, the "white-robed Benedictines," follow it more strictly than do the black-robed Benedictines. The well-known Trappist monks, a branch of the Cistercians, after their names write "O.C.S.O.," meaning the "Order of Cistercians of the Strict Observance." These monks eat the simplest of foods. In the fields, shops, or offices of the monastery where they work to earn a living, the monks avoid needless conversation. Each day and night, including the wee hours of the morning, they spend time in reading and prayer. It is a challenging but rewarding life, both for the body and for the soul.

Abbot Bernard, it is said, "carried the twelfth century on his shoulders." He would have preferred to stay at home in his monastery and teach his monks by word and example how to pray and how to work for the Lord. But almost daily visitors, from princes to poor folk, arrived at the monastery to seek advice from the Doctor Mellifluous, or the "Honey-sweet Teacher," as he was sometimes called. Bernard would listen carefully to every request. Many weeks he would travel from the monastery to help Church and civic leaders find solutions to problems that faced parishes, dioceses, cities, and states. Popes, kings, and bishops asked for his help. "They do not leave me even time to pray," lamented Bernard.

In the year 1130 Bernard convinced the kings and queens of many countries in Europe to support the rightful Pope, Innocent II. In that year, someone who pretended to be Pope, a man named Anacletus II, had gained some recognition in Europe. Later, Pope Innocent assigned Bernard the important duty as the official preacher for the Second Crusade. Bernard could preach a powerful sermon, and the Pope knew that he could convince thousands of soldiers and pilgrims to form armies and march to Palestine to fight and set free from Moslem control the Holy Places where Jesus had lived. Bernard's preaching rallied armies of Christians to support this cause, but the crusade failed and Bernard was wrongfully blamed. The crusaders had turned to robbing, murdering, and unruly behavior, killing thousands of innocent people.

Bernard had a gift which many deeply religious people do not possess. He could communicate to others his religious experiences, his thoughts at prayer. Men joined the Cistercians of Clairvaux because they wanted to pray and to serve God and one another as did Abbot Bernard. To this day people read his books and letters to appreciate his understanding of the spiritual life. Bernard was a talented leader and a holy monk.

Bernard died in 1153, having served thirty-eight years as the abbot of Clairvaux. During those years his monastery sent monks to establish sixty-eight new monasteries from Ireland to Germany. Abbot Bernard was buried at Clairvaux, but in 1790 his relics were brought to the French community of Ville-sous-la-Feste.

It did not take long for the Church leaders to realize that Abbot Bernard's holiness and leadership deserved special honors. In 1174 Pope Alexander III proclaimed Bernard a saint. Seven centuries later, in 1830, Pope Pius VIII named him a Doctor of the Church —a title given to a great teacher of the truths of the Church.

St. Bernard, whose emblem is a beehive, is the patron of beekeepers. He is also the patron of candlemakers, of Liguria, a region in northern Italy, and of Gibralter, the tiny country off the southern coast of Spain.

ST. THOMAS AQUINAS

SUMMA THEO-LOGICA

St. Thomas Aquinas

People who met the Dominican friar Thomas Aquinas face-to-face probably never forgot him. They might remember his brilliant lectures given at thirteenth-century universities. They would be amazed at his wisdom and knowledge. They might remember his size. There is a story told that the dining room of the friary where Thomas lived had a table with a half-moon shaped section cut out of it to accommodate his huge frame. They would also remember Thomas' quiet manner and his concern for others.

St. Thomas Aquinas

b. about 1225
d. March 7, 1274
the "Angelic Doctor"
Patron of Catholic schools

Feast Day — January 28

For other name forms of Thomas, *see* story about St. Thomas More on p. 89.

Thomas was a holy as well as a brilliant man. The Church calls him the Angelic Doctor. In 1567 Pope Pius V named this great teacher of Christian truths a Doctor of the Church. A famous artist has pictured St. Thomas standing in the center of a group of other Doctors of the Church. There he is teaching the teachers. In 1880 Pope Leo XIII named this master teacher the patron of all Catholic schools—from grade schools to universities.

Thomas was born in a castle midway between Rome and Naples in southern Italy about the year 1225. Landulph, his father, was the count of Aquino. At that time southern Italy was part of the kingdom of Sicily. When Thomas was about six years old, his parents brought him to live with the Benedictine monks at the abbey of Monte Cassino. They hoped that Thomas would eventually become a monk, and perhaps some day even the abbot, of that important monastery.

In 1239 Sicily experienced considerable unrest and much fighting. Since soldiers occupied Monte Cassino, the abbot thought it best to send Thomas to Naples for his safety and for more schooling. There in that large city Thomas attended the university, where he did very well in his studies. He also learned much about the lifestyle of the Dominican friars, an Order which had been founded by St. Dominic just thirty years earlier. Thomas wanted to teach the Good News as a Dominican, living very simply on whatever the people would give him. At age nineteen Thomas received the white robe of a Dominican friar.

In Aquino, however, Thomas' mother was very angry that her son had joined an Order of men who had to beg for their living. She told Rinaldo, Thomas' older brother and a soldier, to bring Thomas home. In the meantime Thomas' Dominican superiors had rushed him from

Naples to Rome, with plans to send him on to Paris or Cologne for school. Rinaldo caught up with Thomas near Bologna in northern Italy and brought him home to Aquino.

For the next two years Thomas was a prisoner of his own family, who kept him locked up in a tower. Only his sister visited him. Thomas passed the time by reading books and by learning much of the Bible by heart. Despite his mother's objections, Thomas was determined to remain a Dominican. Finally, in 1245, his proud mother, the countess of Teano, gave up trying to persuade Thomas to change his mind. Both Emperor Frederick, who was related to Thomas, and Pope Innocent IV told the countess that she was wrong. Thomas' solitary confinement was over.

For the next few years Thomas studied at Cologne, Germany, and at Paris, France. One of his teachers was the famous Dominican Albertus Magnus or "Albert the Great," now also a saint. At first Thomas' classmates nicknamed this quiet lad with the build of a professional football player the "dumb Sicilian ox." It was not long, however, before his friends knew that Thomas was anything but dumb. They discovered that Thomas was brilliant—he knew several languages; he knew much about the Bible; he could speak and write clearly; he was familiar with astronomy, geometry, music, and other subjects. Thomas could outscore them in many a test. When Albertus Magnus heard about that nickname, he told his students, "Do not make any mistake. Thomas' bellowing voice will be heard throughout the world."

About 1250 Thomas was ordained a priest by the archbishop of Cologne. His first assignment was to preach the Word of God in Germany, France, and Italy. Then, about 1252, his superiors sent him to Paris to fill an important position in a Dominican school. At that time there was much fighting in Paris at the university over who could and who could not teach. For a while the authorities did not want the Dominicans or the Franciscans teaching at that university. But in June, 1256, Thomas, guarded by soldiers, presented his first lecture as a "master" at that university.

It did not take long before students as well as teachers recognized that Thomas was brilliant. In fact, he surpassed his own teacher, Albertus Magnus, in wisdom and talent. That year Thomas was granted a "doctorate," the highest academic honor at the university. Degrees during the thirteenth century were awarded to students who not only had learned a subject thoroughly but who could also teach it competently.

For the next eighteen years until he died, Thomas served his Order and his Church as a teacher, preacher, counselor, author, and administrator. On many days he lectured in the mornings and answered the students' questions in the afternoons. He taught at several schools in Italy. He was in charge of a *studium* or school in Rome. For a year he advised Pope Urban IV. He helped organize a plan of study for friars who had just joined the Dominicans. He was an expert on the philosophers, men and women of wisdom who had lived centuries earlier, especially Aristotle of Greece.

Thomas wrote with distinction on a variety of subjects. He wrote sermons; he wrote on the Gospels, on the Our Father and the Hail Mary, on theology and philosophy, on the Mass, on the sacraments. He composed hymns, including *O Salutaris Hostia* and *Tantum Ergo,* hymns which have been sung at Catholic services for centuries. Thomas' writings would fill at least twenty thick books.

Fortunately, Thomas had secretaries to help him write down his thoughts. Thomas himself had terrible handwriting. Students in the 1980s still study his books as they did in the 1280s. No one has written on theology, the study of God, more thoroughly or with more wisdom than did Thomas Aquinas. He spent his life answering the question "Who is God?" and helping others answer that same question.

For five years Thomas worked on his greatest book, the *Summa Theologica.* Thomas considered it to be a manual of Christian doctrine, a student's textbook. But it is much more than that. This masterpiece is an elaborate study of ten thousand questions about

God and the meaning of life that God has given to us. Thomas quoted from nineteen councils or meetings of the Church's bishops, from forty-one popes, and fifty-two Fathers of the Church. The *Summa* explains the sacraments, the Mass, the life of Jesus, and numerous other subjects.

Thomas never finished his *Summa*. In 1273, when he was writing on the sacrament of reconciliation, Thomas suddenly put away his pen. He told his friend Father Reginald that he "could not go on. . . . All that I have written seems to me to be like so much straw compared to what I have seen and what was revealed to me."

Thomas Aquinas is remembered not only for his knowledge, teaching skills, and books, but also for his holiness. He was a modest person. He shared his talents willingly with others. He once said that "communicating one's thoughts to others is a greater thing than merely thinking."

In 1274 Pope Gregory X invited Thomas to Lyons, France, to meet with the bishops. On that journey from Naples to Lyons, Thomas became sick and stopped to rest at a monastery at Fossanuova, Italy. There he did not recover his health. The huge man with the brilliant mind was dying. On March 7 that year Thomas died and was buried at that Cistercian monastery. He was not yet fifty years old. Few men have accomplished so much in such a short time.

In 1323 at Avignon, France, where the Pope then lived, His Holiness John XXII with exceptional solemnity canonized Thomas a saint. The Pope said that Thomas deserved to be a saint because of his great life of teaching and defending the Church and because of his holiness. A cardinal said that Thomas is "the most saintly among the learned and the most learned among the saints."

Many years passed before Thomas' Dominican brothers received permission from Pope Urban V to bring the saint's body to one of their friaries. In 1369 the Dominicans carried his remains to a church in Toulouse, France. There, in 1628, a magnificent shrine was dedicated to the saint's honor, but it was destroyed during the French Revolution a century and a half later. St. Thomas' body was then removed to the Cathedral of St. Sernin in Toulouse. There it now lies buried in a casket of gold and silver.

St. Catherine of Siena

St. Catherine grew up in Siena, a city in west central Italy in a region called Tuscany. She never had trouble finding a playmate, since she had twenty-four brothers and sisters. Giacomo Benicasa, her father, and his wife Lapa loved all their children dearly, especially Catherine, the youngest. Giacomo, a wool-dyer, businessman, and politician, was a prominent citizen of Siena.

Like most parents, Giacomo and Lapa wanted Catherine to marry eventually and to raise her own family, but Catherine decided as a little girl not to marry. Rather, she wanted to work with the poor and

St. Catherine of Siena

b. 1347

d. 1380

Patron of Italy
Doctor of the Church

Feast Day — April 29

For other name forms of Catherine, *see* story about Blessed Kateri Tekakwitha on p. 12.

the sick as a Dominican *tertiary*. Such a man or a woman, either single or married, lives in part the life of a religious , but not in a convent or a monastery. Catherine hoped that her parents would understand that she wanted to remain at home and spend time each day helping the poor and the sick families in the neighborhood. In Catherine's day most nuns scarcely ever left their convents, where they lived quiet, prayerful lives.

Catherine had beautiful golden hair, while most girls in Tuscany had jet black hair. To show her parents that she did not want to marry, Catherine cut off her golden hair. Nevertheless, Giacomo and Lapa still objected to Catherine's plans and made her work as the family's maid. They hoped that by having to work hard day and night their daughter would change her mind about becoming a tertiary. Thus, for that large family Catherine served the meals, scrubbed the floors, and did one chore after the other from dawn to dusk.

As time went on Giacomo and Lapa realized that Catherine wanted more than anything else to join the Dominicans. Somewhat reluctantly they gave their permission and Catherine, then sixteen years old, became a tertiary. She now wore the white clothes of a Dominican, but she still lived at home with her family.

It was not long before Giacomo and Lapa had reason once more to worry about their youngest child. They noticed that Catherine spent most of her time in her room praying to God. "Prayer," Catherine said, "was being restless with a tremendous desire for God." She slept little and ate only the simplest foods, mainly bread and raw vegetables. This prayerful seclusion was preparing Catherine for im-

St. CATHERINE of Siena

portant work ahead. After three years she changed her lifestyle dramatically. Each morning she went out into the streets of Siena to begin her rounds of helping the sick and the poor recover their health and complete their daily chores.

In time Catherine also used her talents to serve the important and the mighty of Italy and France. She had a way with words, both as a speaker and a writer, though she never learned these skills in school. Others wrote the letters that she dictated. Catherine wrote to princes, bishops, cardinals, and even the Pope about what she thought the French and Italian governments must do to bring peace. Europe was then plagued by many wars. Important people listened to Catherine.

Catherine wrote six letters to Pope Gregory XI in Avignon, France, where the popes had lived for seventy years. She urged him to return to Rome, which for centuries had been the residence of the popes. She told the Holy Father, "These people who are trying to convince you to remain in France are just looking out for their own interests. Don't be afraid to do what you know is right." Pope Gregory was impressed by Catherine's letters, agreed to meet with her, and after their visit decided to follow her advice. His decision to return to Rome affected the governments of many European nations. Catherine's advice to the Holy Father helped bring peace to that continent.

Though Catherine worked from morning to night in the Siena neighborhoods, she was never too busy each day to pray. One day God sent her a special gift called the stigmata. From then on at certain times there appeared in her body the wounds which Jesus suffered in his hands, feet, and side before he died on the cross. In a special way Catherine shared Christ's wounds.

Catherine was a holy woman who endured much criticism and hardships from others, including her own family. Yet she lived the life of a nun who worked in the world. She was centuries ahead of her time. St. Catherine's lifestyle gave her the opportunity to do special work for God's people.

St. Catherine of Siena is the patron of Italy and nursing. She is also a Doctor of the Church.

St. Teresa of Ávila

Teresa traveled so far and wide throughout her native Spain that the people called her the roving nun. Teresa was a woman of prayer and a talented writer and leader. The Spaniards so dearly loved this holy sister that in 1617 they proclaimed her the patron of their country. A few years later, in 1622, the Church canonized her a saint. More recently she has been named a Doctor of the Church, the first woman to be so honored. Neither Spain, the Church, nor the entire world would ever forget this woman of God.

Teresa Sánchez de Cepeda y Ahumada was born in 1515 in Ávila, Spain. Her father's name was Alonzo Sánchez de Cepeda, her mother's Beatriz Dávila Ahumada. Children's names in Spain to this day often include the last names of both parents. But despite her long name, St. Teresa is better known today simply by her first name and the name of the city she lived most of her life.

St. Teresa of Ávila

b. **March 28, 1515**

d. **October 4, 1582**

Founder of the Discalced Carmelites

Doctor of the Church

Feast Day — October 15

Meaning of name — harvester, from the Greek *therismos* (harvest)

Latin	English
Theresia	**Teresa**
	Theresa
French	**Therese**
Thérèse	**Theres**
Spanish, Italian	**Theresina**
Teresa	**Teresita**
	Terry
Portuguese	**Terri**
Theresa	**Tess**
German	**Tessa**
Theresa	**Tessie**
Theresia	**Jessie**
	Resi
	Tracy

At age twenty Teresa joined a convent of sisters called Carmelites in Ávila. But unfortunately she became seriously sick a few years later. Her father, now a widower, took her from doctor to doctor in several Spanish cities, seeking medical help for his daughter, one of his ten children. That sickness, which might have been malaria, almost killed Teresa. For three years she could not walk a step. Eventually, however, she regained her health and returned to the Incarnation Convent in Ávila.

Despite her uncertain health, Teresa was a reformer. She was not afraid to make changes when she knew that improvements were possible through prayer, planning, and hard work. Teresa realized that convent life in Spain should change. She wanted the convents to be quiet homes where the nuns shared lives of work and prayer, seeking to know God in all that they did. Teresa knew that the Incar-

ST. TERESA

OF ÁVILA

nation Convent was too large—140 sisters lived there. "Experience has taught me what a house full of women is like," Teresa said. "God preserve us from such a state!"

Also, many women boarders stayed at the convent. The place was more like a hotel than a home for sisters. Further, the nuns could keep their own property. Some came from rich families; some from poor families; they shared little and quarreled far too much; there were far too many hard feelings and unhappy faces at Immaculata. The sisters did not even eat supper together. It was customary for each sister to leave the convent each day and eat meals with her family in Ávila. Only bread was served at Immaculata. The convent needed some reorganization, but who would take charge?

Teresa endured this convent life for twenty-five years. Such a lifestyle no doubt brought Teresa many a headache. (Today St. Teresa is remembered as the patron of those who suffer from headaches.) During those years she tried to convince the Church and the civil authorities in Ávila to let her begin a new convent. Finally, in 1562, she received permission to move with four sisters, one of them her niece, to a new convent, which Teresa called St. Joseph's. There the sisters lived a quiet, prayerful life, sharing their food, working together inside the convent at sewing or some other activity to earn a living. They scarcely ever left St. Joseph's. Each day they prayed for several hours. The sisters wore coarse wool dresses and sandals. Since they did not wear shoes, they came to be known as the Discalced (un-shoed) Carmelites.

Teresa said that the first five years at St. Joseph's were the happiest of her life. There with thirteen sisters she prayed and quietly pursued the work of the Lord. Though Teresa preferred to stay at St. Joseph's and direct her nuns, she knew that convents in other cities should be started or reformed. Between 1567 and 1580 Teresa established fourteen other Discalced Carmelite houses in Spain. One of the houses was a monastery for men who were called the Discalced Brethren.

During these same years Teresa's nuns founded seventeen other convents, each with twenty-one or fewer members. Teresa even returned home to the Incarnation Carmelites at Ávila to be their superior. It wasn't easy work, especially at first when many sisters objected to her reforms. She told them: "Do not be afraid that I will inflict on you a rule you haven't agreed to live by."

Teresa knew that growth in prayer enables a person to enter into intimate contact with God. Teresa learned to communicate with God, not only in spoken prayer but also through silent prayer where one's thoughts are directed to God. The priests who advised Teresa knew that God had given this holy woman a special gift of mental prayer. They told her to write books which explained how she prayed. Thus, in an autobiography and in other books Teresa described how she developed her prayer life. Teresa was close to God. Over the last four hundred years, her writings have taught thousands of others much about how to lift their minds and hearts in prayer to God.

Eventually the Carmelites and the Discalced Carmelites became two separate groups of nuns. King Philip II of Spain helped the Church officials make that distinction. The king recognized the great work of both groups of Carmelites—those who wore shoes and those who did not, those who worked somewhat in the lay world and those who lived apart from it as much as possible.

Today convents of Discalced Carmelites founded by St. Teresa's followers are quietly working for the Lord in nations across the world, including the United States. Long hours each day and night these nuns pray to God, thanking him for the blessings the world has received and asking him for his continued protection on themselves and all people.

St. Teresa died in 1582 at Alba, Spain, where she is buried. She is also known as St. Teresa of Jesus.

St. Francis de Sales

As the oldest of six sons of a French nobleman, Francis de Sales could have been a prominent government official living in a castle. He was invited to join the senate of Savoy, the province in eastern France where his family lived, but he refused. His father wanted him to marry an heiress, a very wealthy woman of high social standing, but he again refused. Though he loved his father and his family dearly, Francis had other plans for his life, plans that his father did not always understand. Francis wanted to be a priest.

Francis grew up amidst much controversy concerning religion. Many Catholics in the late 1500s were joining new denominations that the reformers had begun. The reformers in part misunderstood the Church and often preached false statements about it. People even fought in the streets over which faith was the best. It was a difficult time.

St. Francis de Sales

b. August 21, 1567

d. December 28, 1622

Doctor of the Church

Feast Day — January 24

For other name forms of Francis, see story about St. Frances Xavier Cabrini on p. 24.

After attending schools near his hometown of Annecy, Francis enrolled at the University of Paris. There for six years he studied history, literature, languages, and other subjects that a well-educated person should know thoroughly. He also studied theology and Scripture—the study of God and his sacred writings in the Bible. But still more study was to come. His father then sent Francis for three years of hard work at the University of Padua in Italy. There Francis earned a doctor's degree—the highest accomplishment possible at a university—both in civil and Church law. Francis then began a career as a lawyer, but he still hoped to be a priest. His father continued to oppose his wish.

Francis' cousin Louis de Sales, a priest, helped Francis attain his goal. It so happened that an important position in the diocese of Geneva was then vacant. Louis asked the bishop of Geneva, Claude de Granier, to ask the Holy Father to appoint Francis to this important position of provost. The provost was the leader of the priests who lived and worked at the cathedral. Sure enough, the Pope made that appointment. Francis' prominent father, the lord of Nouvelles and Boissy, then gave his consent for Francis to be ordained. Only a priest could be a provost. Thus Francis, who had already studied the subjects which a priest is expected to know, was ordained in 1593.

Francis served as the provost for but one year. In 1594 the duke of

St. Francis De Sales

Savoy was concerned that reformers called Calvinists were urging many Catholics to join that new faith. He asked the bishop of Geneva, whose cathedral city was Annecy, where Francis grew up, to send some well-trained priests to Savoy. The duke hoped that effective preaching and the priests' good example would convince the people, especially those in the area called Chablais along the southern shore of Lake Geneva, to return to the Catholic religion. Francis was the perfect priest for the assignment. He was well trained and already had a reputation as a preacher whom people really listened to. He said yes to Bishop de Granier's call.

The next four years for the young Father de Sales brought some fearsome challenges. The mountain country was wild and dangerous. His father worried that Francis would be killed by angry mobs or by bandits. Indeed, twice Francis was stopped by men who tried to kill him, but he escaped. Once he was attacked by wolves and spent the night perched in a tree. Despite such dangers, Francis went from hamlet to hamlet preaching to small groups, visiting Catholic families, answering the challenges of the reformers, and seeking converts.

Since preaching was not always the best means to teach people, Francis tried a new tactic. He wrote short articles about the beliefs of the Church and distributed the pamphlets to the people. There in black and white the people could study the truths. It was an effective tool, something new that worked. Slowly but surely hundreds of the citizens of Chablais returned to Catholicism. They respected Francis for his learning, holiness, and concern for their souls. Bishop de Granier sent more priests to help Francis. Also the duke of Savoy donated money to rebuild churches and to start Catholic schools. In only two years Francis had made over eight thousand converts.

In 1599 Pope Clement VIII appointed Francis as the coadjutor bishop of Geneva. That meant that when Bishop de Granier died Francis would take his place. That event happened three years later, in 1602. Bishop de Sales accomplished much as the chief pastor of the diocese of Geneva. He opened a seminary to educate young men to be priests. He called his priests together for a meeting once a year to listen to their advice as well as to give them instruction. He organized catechism classes in his parishes, which were scattered up and down the Alpine mountain valleys. He even taught some classes himself. Francis believed in a simple preaching style and a simple lifestyle. Even though he was a bishop, he lived as simply as he could and gave what he did not need to the poor.

Francis' preaching and writing became well known far beyond his diocese. Even King Henry IV praised his sermons and asked him to preach during one Lent in Paris, the French capital. The bishop's book *Introduction to the Devout Life,* which tells how someone who lives amidst the hustle and bustle of the daily world may lead a holy life, was a best seller. In fact, Francis' many and powerful writings convinced Pope Pius XI three hundred years later to name St. Francis de Sales as the patron of journalists, men and women who make their living as writers of newspapers, magazines, and periodicals.

Bishop de Sales is also remembered as the co-founder of the Order of the Visitation. In 1602 at Dijon, France, Francis and the holy woman Jane de Chantal, now also a saint, founded an Order of women to care for the sick and the poor. The Visitation sisters remind us of the Blessed Virgin who visited her kinswoman Elizabeth and took care of her until after her son John the Baptist was born. Bishop de Sales said that the Visitation sisters would be "an Order where the charity and gentleness of Jesus Christ shall rule, where the weak and infirm can be admitted, which shall care for the sick and visit the poor."

In 1622, when Bishop de Sales was but fifty-six years old, he became terribly sick when traveling with the duke of Savoy to meet the French king Louis XIII. Francis died on December 28 that year in Lyons.

In 1665 Pope Alexander VII canonized Francis de Sales. In 1877 Pope Pius IX, in a tribute to this saint's wisdom, learning, and holiness, named him a Doctor of the Church. He is sometimes called the Gentleman Saint.

St. Robert Bellarmine

Robert Bellarmine grew up in Tuscany, a province in west central Italy, where his father was a judge. Vincent Bellarmine hoped that his son would study medicine, but Robert, though he respected his father's interest in his career, had other plans. He decided to join the Jesuit Order and become a priest. Little did either Bellarmine know that centuries later Robert would be remembered as a Doctor of the Church.

Robert lived during the Reformation, a time when the reformers were attacking the structure and the truths of the Church. He knew much about the Bible and about the beliefs and the history of the Church. Robert was also a superb speaker and writer. Thus his superiors asked him to use his talents to correct the reformers.

For the next many years Robert put his every energy into that assignment, studying and preaching about the truths of the Church. Eventually all this research was published in a lengthy book

St. Robert Bellarmine

b. October 4, 1542
d. September 17, 1621

Doctor of the Church

Feast Day — September 17

Meaning of name — bright in fame, from the Old German *hrodperht*

Latin	*English*
Robertus	**Robert**
French	**Robley**
	Bob
Robert	**Bobby**
Spanish, Portuguese	**Rob**
	Dob
Roberto	**Dobbin**
Italian	**Nod**
Roberto	**Hob**
Ruberto	**Nobby**
German	**Bert**
	Pop
Ruprecht	**Robin** m., f.
Rupert	**Bobbie** f.
Ruperta f.	**Roberta**
Norwegian	
Robert	

called the *Controversies.* It did not take long before this book was widely read by Catholics and non-Catholics alike throughout Europe. It gave a detailed and fair account of how problems and misunderstandings about the teachings of the Church developed and how they could be solved. Copies were even smuggled to England, where Catholics were then cruelly persecuted, and sold secretly. During Robert's lifetime alone, twenty editions of the *Controversies* were published.

Among Robert's other writings is a short book of questions and answers about the Church written for children. This catechism was translated into forty languages. For over two hundred years it helped children prepare their lessons about the sacraments, the celebrations, and the beliefs of the Church.

161

DEFENDER
OF THE
FAITH

ST. ROBERT BELLARMINE

A good part of Robert's career involved classroom teaching. Once his Jesuit superiors assigned him to teach Greek to high school students. Robert, however, at that time knew no Greek; he scarcely could write the letters of the complicated Greek alphabet. Nevertheless, night by night he studied that language, keeping a lesson or two ahead of his patient students. In time Robert, as well as many of his students, mastered that language.

As a teacher Robert relied on his wit, his careful preparation, his concern for the other person, and his love of learning to encourage his students to study. Unlike many teachers of his day, he saw no reason to whip a youngster who did poorly on a test or in an assignment.

In preaching homilies Robert had the knack for explaining complicated truths in simple language. Those who listened to him preach about the sacraments, the Mass, and the life of Jesus followed his explanations with some ease. Robert could understand the needs of his listeners and talk in their language. But since he was a short man, at times Robert could barely be seen in the pulpit or speaker's box. In sixteenth-century churches, the pulpit often extended several feet above the heads of the congregation. If Robert noticed that the people were struggling to see him as he preached, he would stand on a stool, which he set on the floor of the pulpit.

Throughout his career Robert worked for five popes in various offices in the Vatican. It was Pope Clement VIII who named Robert a cardinal, a prince of the Church. "There is no one who equals him in learning in the Church of God," said Pope Clement. For three years Robert served as the archbishop of Capua, a city in southern Italy, but then the Pope called him back to a position in Rome. Though he was never elected pope, Robert is remembered as an authority on the duties, responsibilities, and powers of the Holy Father.

Robert lived simply, even as an archbishop and cardinal. Although his duties in Rome demanded that he live in an apartment right in the Vatican close to the Holy Father, he kept his household expenses to the bare minimum. Like the poor of Italy in the sixteenth century, he ate little else but bread and garlic. It had to be a bitterly cold January evening before he would light a fire in his stove. Robert took down the drapes and the cloth wall coverings from his apartment and gave them to the poor to sew into jackets and coats. "The walls won't catch cold," he said. When a soldier who deserted from the army needed to be ransomed, Robert provided the money. Robert possessed a big heart and a brilliant mind.

In his later years Robert retired to a monastery, where he had spent his first years as a religious. Through prayer he prepared for a holy death, which, despite a lifetime of ill health, did not come to him until age seventy-nine.

It was a pope of this century, Pius XI, who in 1930 declared Robert Bellarmine a saint. The next year Pope Pius honored him with the title "Doctor of the Church." The name Robert means "bright in fame." Indeed, St. Robert Bellarmine's fame brightened the Church and the world in the sixteenth century and to this day.

APPENDICES

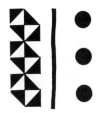
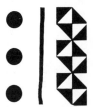

Glossary

ABBOT: the monk elected by his brother monks to be their leader. The monks call him "Father Abbot."

APOSTLE: from the Greek word for messenger *(apostolos)*, generally refers to one of the twelve special disciples of Jesus. Jesus selected, trained, and directed the apostles to preach the message of his gospel, to baptize, and to establish, direct, and care for his Church. They were the first bishops of the Church. The original twelve apostles were: Peter, Andrew, James the Greater, John, Philip, Bartholomew, Thomas, Matthew, James the Less, Jude, Simon, and Judas Iscariot. After Jesus' ascension to heaven, the apostles elected Matthias to take the place of Judas.

The term also refers to St. Paul, the "Apostle to the Gentiles," and to St. Barnabas, who worked closely with St. Paul as a missionary.

ASIA MINOR: a peninsula in west Asia between the Black and the Mediterranean Seas, including most of Turkey. Some of the apostles preached the gospel to the people who lived here. The important city of Constantinople (now Istanbul) is located on the ribbon of water called the Bosporus which connects the Black Sea and the Sea of Marmara, which leads to the Mediterranean.

BEATIFICATION: a major step toward being canonized a saint of the Church. At a ceremony, usually at St. Peter's Basilica in the Vatican, the Holy Father declares that a particular candidate for sainthood, an individual of pronounced heroic virtue, is a *beatus (beata,* f.) or a blessed person.

BIBLE: the most important book ever written, since it is the Word of God. To many authors God gave special talents to write the seventy-three books that make up the Bible, which has two main divisions, the Old Testament and the New Testament.

The Old Testament contains forty-six books and the New Testament twenty-seven. The Old Testament or the Hebrew Scriptures tell about the creation of the world, the sin of Adam and Eve, the promise of God to send a Messiah, and the life of God's Chosen People, the Jews or the Hebrew people, as they awaited the Redeemer. The Jews, who regarded Jesus as a great prophet but not as the Redeemer, are still awaiting the coming of the Savior.

The New Testament describes the years that Jesus, the Son of God and the Redeemer, lived on this earth in the Holy Land and how his death on the cross fulfilled God's promise to redeem the human race. It also describes the first years of the Church that Jesus left to the direction of the apostles.

Among the famous people written about in the books of the Bible are Judith, Jonathan, Joseph, Moses, Abraham, Isaac, Daniel, Samuel, Isaiah, Ruth, Jeremiah, Rebecca, and Noah (Old Testament) and Peter, John, Paul, the Blessed Virgin, James, Timothy, Pontius Pilate, King Herod, Nicodemus, and Jesus, the Son of God (New Testament).

BISHOP: a priest who is ordained to the fullness of the sacrament of holy orders and thus becomes a successor to the apostles. The Church has about three thousand bishops across the world, most of whom govern a diocese, which is a group of parishes. The Pope is the chief bishop of the Church. On a regular basis the bishop of a diocese, or a bishop who assists him, visits the parishes of the diocese to celebrate the sacrament of confirmation or to meet with the clergy and the parishioners. The bishop is the chief pastor of the diocese.

BROTHER: usually the term refers to a man who is not a priest but who belongs to a religious Order. Some Orders, such as the Franciscans and the Benedictines, have both brothers and priests in their membership. Other Orders, such as the Christian Brothers and the Alexian Brothers, do not have priests in their membership. The Christian Brothers are teachers in schools and colleges. The Alexian Brothers care for the sick.

CANONIZATION: the final step in naming a saint of the Church. After the Church authorities are convinced that a person of heroic virtue is in heaven with God (and should be imitated), the Pope at St. Peter's Basilica in the Vatican during a solemn ceremony declares that the blessed person is a saint.

CARDINAL: one of the counselors to the Pope, a member of the Sacred College of Cardinals. The cardinals, about 120 in number, advise the Pope, head important offices of the Church, and frequently are bishops of dioceses. A cardinal is addressed as "Eminence." At the ceremony of admission to the college, the Pope gives the new cardinal a red biretta—a hard, somewhat square cap—which is a major symbol of his office. (Formerly, until 1969, the cardinal received a broad-brimmed red hat with a low crown and two clusters of fifteen tassels. This hat was not worn again, but upon the cardinal's death was suspended over his tomb or from the rafters of his cathedral.)

When the Pope dies, the cardinals gather in Rome for his funeral. A few days later the cardinals under age eighty then meet in the Vatican's Sistine Chapel at a secret session called a conclave. There they elect one of their number as the next Pope.

CATHEDRAL: the chief church of a diocese, usually located in the city from which the diocese takes its name. The cathedral is the bishop's church. Often cathedrals are huge churches built with expensive materials (granite, stained glass, etc.). The most famous cathedral in the United States is St. Patrick's Cathedral in New York City. The oldest cathedral in the United States is St. Louis Cathedral in New Orleans. In the sanctuary of each cathedral is a special chair reserved for the bishop. Occasionally the bishop comes to the cathedral to celebrate Mass or to preside at special ceremonies, such as the ordination of a priest or the blessing of the holy oils.

CENTURY: a period of one hundred years. The first year of Jesus' life is counted as A.D. 1 or 1 A.D. *A.D.* means *Anno Domini* or "year of the Lord." The years before Jesus' birth are designated B.C. ("before Christ"), or B.C.E. ("before the Christian era"). Thus, Jesus lived during the first century A.D. The 1980s, then, are in the twentieth century A.D.

CONSTANTINOPLE: former name of the city in Turkey now known as Istanbul. It also was once named Byzantium. The city was named after Constantine the Great, the first Christian emperor of Rome (301–337).

CONVENT: the home of a group of sisters or nuns

DEACON: a man who is ordained to the first degree of ministry in the sacrament of holy orders, a step called the diaconate. Deacons may be either candidates for the priesthood, who in another year or so will be ordained as priests, or they may be permanent deacons who will not become priests. In 1964 the Second Vatican Council approved the restoration of the permanent diaconate, a position that was common in the early centuries of the Church. Permanent deacons may be single or married.

"Deacon" originates from the Greek word *diakonos*, which means "servant" or "helper." Deacons are ordained to serve the people of God in three areas—the ministry of the Word (proclaiming the gospel at Mass and preaching its message), the ministry of liturgy (such duties as being an ordinary minister of Communion, solemnly administering the sacrament of baptism, witnessing and blessing marriages, and officiating at wakes, funerals, and burial services), and the ministry of charity (visiting the sick, teaching, social work, administrative duties in Church offices, etc.).

A deacon is addressed as "Mister." At Mass or other church services the deacon is usually vested in a white alb and wears a stole diagonally left to right across his body.

DIOCESE: in the Church a territory of many parishes under the leadership of a bishop, who is known as the Ordinary of the diocese. Across the world the Church is divided into dioceses, much like a country is divided into states.

DISCIPLE: one of the early followers of Jesus during his public life. St. Luke's Gospel (chapter 10) tells us that Jesus sent out seventy-two disciples, two-by-two, to preach the gospel throughout the Holy Land.

DOCTOR OF THE CHURCH: a title given by the Pope to a saint who was a very important writer or teacher of the truths of the Church. Among the saints so honored by this title are Jerome, Gregory the Great, Bernard of Clairvaux, Robert Bellarmine, Teresa of Ávila, Thomas Aquinas, and Francis de Sales.

EVANGELIST: any one of the major authors associated with the four Gospels: Matthew, Mark, Luke, and John.

FEAST DAY: a day set aside by the Church to celebrate the memory of a saint or saints or a mystery of faith such as the Trinity.

FRIAR: a member of a mendicant Order such as the Franciscans or the Dominicans. "Mendicant" means beggar. Originally the mendicant Orders did not own property. Each day the friars would work among the people—preaching, teaching, doing parish work. They would depend on gifts from the people to support themselves. At night the friars would return home to their friary. In contrast, monks, who like friars are religious following a rule established by their founder, generally both live and work in the place of their residence, which is called a monastery.

GOSPELS: the first four books of the New Testament, the second major division of the Bible. The Gospels describe Jesus' life on this earth and the founding of his Church. A reading from one of the Gospels is proclaimed at every Mass.

HERESY: a religious belief that is in opposition to the official teaching of an established Church. For example, around the year 400 an English monk named Pelagius taught, among other errors, that there is no original sin. Pelagianism was condemned by the bishops in 431 at the Council of Ephesus, the third ecumenical council.

HOLY LAND: a common name for Israel, the country where Jesus lived while on this earth and the homeland of the Jewish or Hebrew people. The Hebrews, known also as the Israelites, at God's command were led from Egypt by Moses, Aaron, and Joshua to Israel, the Promised Land. Its three regions—Galilee, Samaria, and Judea—were governed by the Romans during the time of Jesus. Sometimes Israel is called Palestine, a territory which since 1948 includes the State of Israel and the State of Jordan, with the Gaza Strip administered by Egypt.

HOLY RULE: the little book of seventy-three chapters written by St. Benedict in the sixth century to guide his monks in their life of prayer and work. Other founders of religious Orders often based the rules they prepared for their members on St. Benedict's *Holy Rule.*

JEW: a member of the Chosen People of God to whose nation the Redeemer of the world was born. That Redeemer was Jesus, but the Jews or the Hebrews never accepted him as such, since they were expecting the Redeemer to be a powerful earthly king. The homeland of the Jewish people is the nation of Israel, but Jewish people live all over the world.

MARTYR: a person who dies rather than give up his or her faith. The word *martyr* means witness. A martyr, then, is a "witness to Jesus and his Church." During the first three centuries of the Church, thousands of Christians were martyred by the Romans and others who would not tolerate them. In every century since then, Christians have been martyred. For example, in 1597, six Franciscans, three Jesuits, and seventeen Japanese laymen called the Twenty-six Holy Martyrs were crucified for their faith in Nagasaki, Japan. Between 1642 and 1649 six Jesuit missionary priests and their two assistants were martyred by Indians in upstate New York and Canada.

MONK: a man who belongs to a religious Order and lives with other monks in a home called a monastery. Monks may be either priests, men who are ordained, or brothers, men who are not ordained. The leader or father of the monks is a priest called an abbot. Monks gather several times each day in their monastery chapel to pray together.

NOVICE: a man or woman in the trial period (usually one or two years) as a member of a religious Order. During that period the novice learns how to live the life of a religious.

NUN: a woman who belongs to a religious Order, particularly one who lives apart from the world in a convent, much as a monk does in a monastery. A nun is more commonly known as a sister. Sisters, unlike nuns, generally work outside their convents in parishes, schools, hospitals, etc.

OBLATE: *See* **TERTIARY.**

PATRON SAINT: a saint who is especially remembered by the people of a certain part of the world, country, job, activity, or cause. For example, the Blessed Virgin, under the title of Our Lady of Guadalupe, is the patron of the Americas; St. Patrick, of Ireland; St. Simon the Apostle, of tanners and woodcutters; St. Bernard of Clairvaux, of beekeepers and candlemakers; St. Anthony of Padua, for help in finding lost items.

POPE: the leader of the Catholic Church. Jesus appointed St. Peter to lead the other apostles and the early Christians. Pope John Paul II in 1978 became the 265th Pope to lead the Church. Among the Pope's many titles are "the bishop of Rome," "Servant of the Servants of God," "Vicar of Jesus Christ," and "Supreme Pontiff of the Universal Church." The Pope is familiarly known as the Holy Father. When the Pope dies, the cardinals of the Church gather in Vatican City for his funeral and then those under age eighty elect one of their number as the next Pope.

PRIEST: a man who is ordained to the second degree of ministry in the sacrament of holy orders to serve the Church. In Jesus' name a priest celebrates Mass, baptizes, forgives sins, blesses marriages, preaches and counsels, anoints the sick, and buries the dead. A bishop ordains a man a priest. That man must first for several years study the Bible, theology, philosophy, and other subjects in a school called a seminary.

RELIC: an object connected with a saint. Relics are divided into three groups or classes: (1) the body of a saint or any part of it, (2) any object that belonged to a saint, such as an article of clothing, and (3) an object touched to the body of a saint. Christians often visit the tomb or grave of a saint to pray for that holy person's intercession with God for a certain cause. Sometimes a part of a saint's body, such as the heart, is kept in a place apart from the tomb of that saint. Thus, several shrines may have a first-class relic of the same saint.

RELIGIOUS ORDER: an organization of priests, brothers, or sisters who serve the Church, such as the Benedictines, Dominicans, Franciscans, etc. The members of an Order follow a rule or a set of regulations established by their founder. An Order often specializes in a certain type of work, such as teaching, parish work, or care of the sick. Some Orders permit lay people to belong to their number as *tertiaries* or *oblates,* that is, members of a "Third Order."

ROMANS: the people and government of the ancient city of Rome, now the capital of Italy, who for over four hundred years (27 B.C. to A.D. 395) ruled most of the known world. The countries ruled by the Roman emperor and his governors, such as Palestine where Jesus lived in the first century, were known as the Roman Empire. In 395 the empire was divided into the Eastern Roman Empire, with the capital at Constantinople, and the Western Roman Empire, with the capital at Rome.

ROME: ancient city, capital of what is now Italy. From 27 B.C. to A.D. 395, Rome was the capital of the powerful Roman Empire and from 395 to 476 the capital of the Western Roman Empire. In 476 the city was destroyed by the Vandals, invaders from northern Europe. From the time of St. Peter, Rome has been the headquarters of the Church. Vatican City, where the Pope lives, is a separate nation inside the city of Rome.

ST. PETER'S BASILICA: the largest church in all Christendom and the most important church of Catholicism. The basilica is located in Vatican City, one of the world's tiniest countries (just 108 acres). It took over 250 years (1506–1776) to construct the basilica, which was designed by Michelangelo, Raphael, Bramante, and other famous Italian architects. Here the Pope celebrates Mass on important occasions and presides at services of the Church. The Pope lives just next door to the basilica.

ST. PETER'S SQUARE: an open area in front of St. Peter's Basilica, which is so huge that it will hold about 250,000 people. 392 pillars in four rows hold up the roof that rings the square. 140 statues of saints are spaced evenly along the roof. The Pope's apartment looks down upon the square. On Sundays at noon the Pope stands at a window and blesses the people gathered in the square.

THE TEMPLE: the main place of worship of the Jewish people in Jerusalem. King Solomon built the first Temple about the year 1000 B.C. In it was a room of great beauty constructed to hold the Ark of the Covenant, an ornate box which held the tablets on which were written the Ten Commandments (which God had given to Moses on Mount Sinai), a golden dish which held some of the manna (which God gave the Israelites to eat when they were in the desert for many years after leaving Egypt), and the rod of Moses' brother Aaron (which had blossomed). For forty years, while the Israelites were in the desert, they carried the ark in procession wherever they went. Finally, in the Promised Land of Israel, the ark was reverently placed in the Temple.

About four hundred years after King Solomon completed the Temple, it was destroyed. But it was rebuilt and expanded. During Jesus' life on earth the Temple was a magnificent structure. It was destroyed again by the Romans about thirty-five years after Jesus died. Today a part of the wall of the Temple which still stands is called the Western Wall. It is a holy place of pilgrimage for the Jewish people.

TERTIARY: a member of a so-called Third Order of a religious Order. Usually the term refers to a lay person—someone who is not a priest, brother, or sister—who in his or her daily life practices the spirit and the prayer life of a particular religious Order as much as possible. Some Orders permit tertiaries to be buried in the habit—the special uniform—that the members of the Order wear. Some Orders (for example, the Benedictines) call a tertiary an *oblate.*

VATICAN CITY: the tiny country (108 acres) inside the city of Rome, Italy, which is the headquarters of the Catholic Church and the home of the Pope and other officials of the Church. St. Peter's Basilica and Square occupy most of the space in this nation.

VENERABLE: a title given a person of God whose candidacy for sainthood has been officially accepted by the Holy Father. The investigation of that person's life then continues. The term comes from the Latin *venerari,* "to revere."

A Calendar of Saints' Feast Days

JANUARY

1 Solemnity of Mary, the Mother of God
2 Basil the Great and Gregory Nazianzen, *bishops and doctors*
4 Elizabeth Ann Seton (United States)
5 John Neumann, *bishop* (United States)
6 Blessed André Bessette, *religious* (United States)
7 Raymond of Penyafort, *priest*
13 Hilary, *bishop and doctor*
17 Antony, *abbot*
20 Fabian, *pope and martyr*
    Sebastian, *martyr*
21 Agnes, *virgin and martyr*
22 Vincent, *deacon and martyr*
24 Francis de Sales, *bishop and doctor*
25 Conversion of Paul, *apostle*
26 Timothy and Titus, *bishops*
27 Angela Merici, *virgin*
28 Thomas Aquinas, *priest and doctor*
31 John Bosco, *priest*

FEBRUARY

2 Presentation of the Lord
3 Blase, *bishop and martyr*
    Ansgar, *bishop*
5 Agatha, *virgin and martyr*
6 Paul Miki and Companions, *martyrs*
8 Jerome Emiliani
10 Scholastica, *virgin*
11 Our Lady of Lourdes
14 Cyril, *monk,* and Methodius, *bishop*
17 Seven Founders of the Order of Servites
21 Peter Damian, *bishop and doctor*
22 Chair of Peter, *apostle*
23 Polycarp, *bishop and martyr*

MARCH

4 Casimir
7 Perpetua and Felicity, *martyrs*
8 John of God, *religious*
9 Frances of Rome, *religious*
17 Patrick, *bishop*
18 Cyril of Jerusalem, *bishop and doctor*
19 Joseph, *husband of Mary*
23 Turibius de Mongrovejo, *bishop*

APRIL

2 Francis of Paola, *hermit*
4 Isidore, *bishop and doctor*
5 Vincent Ferrer, *priest*
7 John Baptist de la Salle, *priest*
11 Stanislaus, *bishop and martyr*
13 Martin I, *pope and martyr*
21 Anselm, *bishop and doctor*
23 George, *martyr*
24 Fidelis of Sigmaringen, *priest and martyr*
25 Mark, *evangelist*
28 Peter Chanel, *priest and martyr*
29 Catherine of Siena, *virgin and doctor*
30 Pius V, *pope*

MAY

1 Joseph the Worker
2 Athanasius, *bishop and doctor*
3 Philip and James (the Less), *apostles*
12 Nereus and Achilleus, *martyrs*
    Pancras, *martyr*
14 Matthias, *apostle*
15 Isidore (United States)
18 John I, *pope and martyr*
20 Bernardine of Siena, *priest*
25 Venerable Bede, *priest and doctor*
    Gregory VII, *pope*
    Mary Magdalene de Pazzi, *virgin*
26 Philip Neri, *priest*
27 Augustine of Canterbury, *bishop*
31 Visitation

JUNE

1 Justin, *martyr*
2 Marcellinus and Peter, *martyrs*

171

3	Charles Lwanga and Companions, *martyrs*	8	Dominic, *priest*
5	Boniface, *bishop and martyr*	10	Lawrence, *deacon and martyr*
6	Norbert, *bishop*	11	Clare, *virgin*
9	Ephrem, *deacon and doctor*	13	Pontian, *pope and martyr,* and Hippolytus, *priest and martyr*
11	Barnabas, *apostle*	15	Assumption
13	Anthony of Padua, *priest and doctor*	16	Stephen of Hungary
19	Romuald, *abbot*	19	John Eudes, *priest*
21	Aloysius Gonzaga, *religious*	20	Bernard, *abbot and doctor*
22	Paulinus of Nola, *bishop*	21	Pius X, *pope*
	John Fisher, *bishop and martyr*	22	Queenship of Mary
	Thomas More, *martyr*	23	Rose of Lima, *virgin*
24	Birth of John the Baptist	24	Bartholomew, *apostle*
27	Cyril of Alexandria, *bishop and doctor*	25	Louis
28	Irenaeus, *bishop and martyr*		Joseph Calasanz, *priest*
29	Peter and Paul, *apostles*	27	Monica
30	First Martyrs of the Church of Rome	28	Augustine, *bishop and doctor*
		29	Beheading of John the Baptist, *martyr*

JULY

3	Thomas, *apostle*
4	Elizabeth of Portugal
5	Anthony Zaccaria, *priest*
6	Maria Goretti, *virgin and martyr*
11	Benedict, *abbot*
13	Henry
14	Blessed Kateri Tekakwitha, *virgin* (United States)
	Camillus of Lellis, *priest*
15	Bonaventure, *bishop and doctor*
16	Our Lady of Mount Carmel
21	Lawrence of Brindisi, *priest and doctor*
22	Mary Magdalene
23	Bridget, *religious*
25	James (the Greater), *apostle*
26	Joachim and Anne, *parents of Mary*
29	Martha
30	Peter Chrysologus, *bishop and doctor*
31	Ignatius of Loyola, *priest*

SEPTEMBER

3	Gregory the Great, *pope and doctor*
8	Birth of Mary
9	Peter Claver, *priest* (United States)
13	John Chrysostom, *bishop and doctor*
15	Our Lady of Sorrows
16	Cornelius, *pope and martyr,* and Cyprian, *bishop and martyr*
17	Robert Bellarmine, *bishop and doctor*
19	Januarius, *bishop and martyr*
21	Matthew, *apostle and evangelist*
26	Cosmas and Damian, *martyrs*
27	Vincent de Paul, *priest*
28	Wenceslaus, *martyr*
29	Michael, Gabriel, and Raphael, *archangels*
30	Jerome, *priest and doctor*

AUGUST

1	Alphonsus Liguori, *bishop and doctor*
2	Eusebius of Vercelli, *bishop*
4	John Vianney, *priest*
7	Sixtus II, *pope and martyr,* and Companions, *martyrs*
	Cajetan, *priest*

OCTOBER

1	Theresa of the Child Jesus, *virgin*
2	Guardian Angels
4	Francis of Assisi
6	Bruno, *priest*
	Blessed Marie-Rose Durocher, *virgin* (United States)
7	Our Lady of the Rosary

9 Denis, *bishop and martyr,* and Companions, *martyrs*
John Leonardi, *priest*
10 Maximilian Kolbe, *martyr*
14 Callistus I, *pope and martyr*
15 Teresa of Ávila, *virgin and doctor*
16 Hedwig, *religious*
Margaret Mary Alacoque, *virgin*
17 Ignatius of Antioch, *bishop and martyr*
18 Luke, *evangelist*
19 Isaac Jogues and John de Brébeuf, *priests, and Companions, martyrs* (United States)
Paul of the Cross, *priest*
23 John of Capistrano, *priest*
24 Anthony Claret, *bishop*
28 Simon and Jude, *apostles*

NOVEMBER

1 All Saints
2 All Souls
3 Martin de Porres, *religious*
4 Charles Borromeo, *bishop*
10 Leo the Great, *pope and doctor*
11 Martin of Tours, *bishop*
12 Josaphat, *bishop and martyr*
13 Frances Xavier Cabrini, *virgin* (United States)
15 Albert the Great, *bishop and doctor*

16 Margaret of Scotland
Gertrude, *virgin*
17 Elizabeth of Hungary, *religious*
21 Presentation of Mary
22 Cecilia, *virgin and martyr*
23 Clement I, *pope and martyr*
Columban, *abbot*
30 Andrew, *apostle*

DECEMBER

3 Francis Xavier, *priest*
4 John Damascene, *priest and doctor*
6 Nicholas, *bishop*
7 Ambrose, *bishop and doctor*
8 Immaculate Conception
11 Damasus I, *pope*
12 Our Lady of Guadalupe (United States)
Jane Frances de Chantal, *religious*
13 Lucy, *virgin and martyr*
14 John of the Cross, *priest and doctor*
21 Peter Canisius, *priest and doctor*
23 John of Kanty, *priest*
26 Stephen, *first martyr*
27 John, *apostle and evangelist*
28 Holy Innocents, *martyrs*
29 Thomas Becket, *bishop and martyr*
31 Sylvester I, *pope*

WHAT NAME? WHAT SAINT?

The stories in this book describe fifty-two saints whose names (including shortened forms) in various languages are given below. The list is by no means complete. The numbers direct the reader to the appropriate story.